Peinture le Chevalier Kneller.                    Gravé par le Chevalier Chéreau C.P.R.

Mr. John Dryden

# All For Love

## JOHN DRYDEN

*Edited by* N. J. ANDREW

LONDON/ERNEST BENN LIMITED

NEW YORK/W. W. NORTON AND COMPANY INC.

*First published in this form 1975*
*by Ernest Benn Limited*
*Sovereign Way, Tonbridge, Kent, TN9 1RW*
*Second impression 1983*

© *Ernest Benn Limited 1975*

*Published in the United States of America by*
*W. W. Norton and Company Inc.*
*500 Fifth Avenue, New York, N.Y. 10110*

*Distributed in Canada by*
*The General Publishing Company Limited · Toronto*

*Printed in Great Britain*

ISBN 0–510–33711–2
ISBN 0–393–90006–1 (U.S.A.)

# CONTENTS

| | |
|---|---|
| Acknowledgements | ix |
| Introduction | xi |
| The Author | xi |
| Sources | xiv |
| The Play | xviii |
| Notes on the Text | xxix |
| Abbreviations | xxx |
| Further Reading | xxx |

ALL FOR LOVE

| | |
|---|---|
| Epistle Dedicatory | 3 |
| Preface | 10 |
| Prologue | 21 |
| Persons represented | 22 |
| The Text | 23 |
| Epilogue | 114 |

# ACKNOWLEDGEMENTS

IN THE PREPARATION of this edition, I have made extensive use of the eighteen-volume *Works* edited by Sir Walter Scott, revised and corrected by George Saintsbury (Edinburgh, 1882–93), *Four Tragedies* edited by L. A. Beaurline and Fredson Bowers (Chicago, 1967), and the Regents Restoration Drama Series *All For Love* edited by David M. Vieth (London, 1973). The biographical note is based primarily on Charles E. Ward's *Life of John Dryden* (Chapel Hill, N.C., 1961).

I would like to thank Professor Brian Morris and Miss Roma Gill of the University of Sheffield for their help and advice.

N. J. ANDREW

# INTRODUCTION

## THE AUTHOR

THE LITERARY CAREER of John Dryden, born in Aldwinkle, North-amptonshire, on 19 August 1631, began in 1649 with the publication of his elegy *Upon the Death of Lord Hastings*. From this time to the Restoration of Charles II in 1660, during which period he graduated from Cambridge University (in 1654) and possibly worked in the civil service, a small number of unremarkable poems survive, of which one, *Heroic Stanzas to the Glorious Memory of Cromwell* (1659), provides an extraordinary contrast to the staunch Royalism which Dryden's poetry from 1660 onwards exhibits. *Astraea Redux* ('a poem on the happy restoration and return of His Sacred Majesty Charles II'), published in 1660, was followed by others culminating in *Annus Mirabilis* (1667), all celebrating Charles II's sovereignty or defending him from the poetic attacks of political opponents as able as Andrew Marvell. Presumably in recognition of such services, Dryden was made Poet Laureate on the death of Sir William Davenant in 1668, and in 1670 he was in addition appointed Historiographer Royal. These posts both carried a stipend (which Dryden experienced difficulty in obtaining, and never received in full) which augmented the income which he had inherited on the death of his father in 1654. Nevertheless, it was probably his need to make a living from his literary work which made him concentrate on playwriting during the early years of the Restoration. His first play, *The Wild Gallant*, a rather weak but intermittently funny comedy first performed in February 1663, was not a success, but a year later he won considerable acclaim with *The Indian Queen*, a tragi-comedy written in collaboration with his brother-in-law Sir Robert Howard, one of the major shareholders in the new King's Company by which Dryden's plays were performed until 1678. In the period from 1664 to 1681, he wrote a further nineteen plays and operas. While only *Amboyna, or the Cruelties of the Dutch to the English Merchants* (1672 or 3) descends to the level of unmitigated hack writing (in this case a crude piece of political propaganda), they are for the most part competent rather than brilliant, although works such as *The Tempest* (1667), *Tyrannic Love* (1669), and *Aureng-Zebe* (1675) have considerable merits, and *The State of Innocence* (published 1677), an attempt to adapt *Paradise Lost* as an opera, deserves attention as an extraordinary and improbable literary curio.

*All For Love* was the second of three plays by Dryden to have a Shakespearean source. The first recorded performance took place at the Theatre Royal, Drury Lane, on 12 December 1677. The company of actors responsible, the King's Company, was one of the two which was granted a patent by Charles II on his restoration. By the time *All For Love* was performed, its fortunes were in decline: its foremost actors, Hart and Mohun, who took the leading male parts in *All For Love* as in most of the company's repertoire, were approaching the end of distinguished careers, and the rival Duke's Company was attracting larger audiences by including spectacular scenic effects in their productions. *All For Love* was in fact the last play which Dryden wrote for the King's Company: his next play, *The Kind Keeper*, was acted at the Dorset Gardens Theatre of the Duke's Company, as were the rest of the plays he wrote before the union of the Companies in 1682.[1]

As Dryden's pre-eminence became more clearly established, his involvement in literary controversy grew. In 1668, his masterly *Of Dramatic Poesy: an Essay* was published, and this was followed by other writings on critical theory which varied in manner from the carefully reasoned tone of the Essay to the outright lampoon of *MacFlecknoe*. His writing in this field tended to carry implications which went beyond the purely critical into the sphere of politics, and as Charles II's position became increasingly insecure in the climate of growing political and religious hysteria which surrounded the notorious Popish Plot, Dryden used his skill as a controversialist to produce the didactic poems and satires on which his modern reputation is primarily based. In 1681 he published *Absalom and Achitophel*, in which his choice of biblical context, once accepted, virtually dictates the reader's sympathy for Charles II, the 'godlike David' of line 14, and condemnation of Charles's main political opponent, Anthony Ashley Cooper, earl of Shaftesbury ('false Achitophel', 1. 150: Dryden's comparison of Shaftesbury to a Miltonic Satan is analogous to his reference to the 'old forefather' of malcontents in the Epistle Dedicatory to *All For Love*). The following year, Shaftesbury was again the object of Dryden's satirical attack, in *The Medal*, which, while scathing, is altogether more conventional than the earlier poem. In 1682 Dryden also produced *Religio Laici*, an anglican apology with strong political overtones. His emphasis in this poem on obedience to authority in religion, as in politics, suggests one reason other than expediency for his announcement of his conversion to Catholicism on the death of Charles II and accession of the Catholic James II in 1685. Two

[1] For details of the theatrical background, see William Van Lennep, *The London Stage, 1660–1800* (Carbondale, Illinois, 1960–65), I.

years later, his new faith was the subject of *The Hind and the Panther*, a lengthy didactic poem in fable form.

While the overall impression of the period of Dryden's life from 1675 to 1688 must be of a growing political and religious commitment, and a desire to use his literary talent to further the ends of the causes he espoused, it must be pointed out that he was producing lyrical poetry of the quality of the *Ode to the Memory of Mrs Anne Killigrew* (1686) and *A Song for St Cecilia's Day, 1687* and also turning his attention to producing, as commercial undertakings, poetical miscellanies, which he both compiled and contributed to.

In 1688 James II was overthrown by William of Orange, and Dryden, because of his beliefs and affiliations, was inevitably deprived of his Poet Laureateship and of the income which went with it. He immediately turned towards those forms of writing which were most commercially viable, miscellanies and plays, of which he wrote four in four years: these tend to bear the mark of hack writing, although *Don Sebastian* (1689; published 1690) is one of his finest dramatic pieces. His scholarship had a strictly utilitarian function in the final ten years of his life, which were mainly occupied with the production on a strongly commercial basis of the translations of the classics: *The Satires of Juvenal and Persius* (1692), in which some of the translations from Juvenal were by other hands, was followed in 1697 by his great translation of Virgil and finally by *Fables Ancient and Modern*, from Homer, Ovid, Chaucer, and Boccaccio, in 1700.

The tone of the few less impersonal writings which he permitted himself in this period tends to be embittered: in 1694 he published a poem to Sir Godfrey Kneller, the most celebrated portrait-painter of the time, in which he gave voice to his frustration:

> Thy genius, bounded by the times like mine,⎫
> Drudges on petty draughts, nor dare design ⎬
> A more exalted work, and more divine: ⎭
> For what a song or senseless opera
> Is to the living labour of a play,
> Or what a play to Virgil's work would be,
> Such is a single piece to history . . .
> Mean time, while just encouragement you want,
> You only paint to live, not live to paint.
>
> (ll. 147–53, 164–5)

Finally, perhaps, he became resigned to the frustrations of writing for a living for people he felt did not appreciate him. On 29 April 1700, his *Secular Masque* was performed as part of Sir John Vanbrugh's *The Pilgrim* (adapted from Fletcher, appropriately).

Here the bitterness is relatively gentle, as he reviews with irony the failures of the past century:

> All, all of a piece throughout:
> Thy chase had a beast in view;
> Thy wars brought nothing about;
> Thy lovers were all untrue.
> 'Tis well an old age is out,
> And time to begin a new.                    (ll. 92–7)

Two days after the first performance Dryden died. He was buried in Westminster Abbey on 13 May 1700.


## SOURCES

Dryden's comment, in the Preface to *All For Love*, that he has 'drawn the character of Antony as favourably as Plutarch, Appian, and Dion Cassius would give [him] leave . . .'[2] makes the search for his classical sources an easy one. A study of these three historians reveals that in one respect this statement is not strictly true: Antony is charged with responsibility for the death of his first wife, Fulvia, (II, 300–1) only by Dio, while Appian imputes a limited degree of guilt to him, and Plutarch mentions her death as a fact dissociated from any action on his part. A further tenuous suggestion of Dryden's debt to Dio's *Roman History* may be found in the same act: Cleopatra's excuse for her flight from battle (II, 376–7) appears to be based on a similarly charitable interpretation placed on it by Dio. There is clearer evidence of Dryden's use of Appian's *Civil Wars*, despite the fact that Appian's narrative ends before Antony's death: in his description of Antony's part in the battle of Philippi (I, 439–446), Dryden uses detail which he could only have found in that work (Book III, chapter 14, 111); neither Plutarch nor Dio even describes the same event.

Each of these instances of Dryden's apparent use of Dio and Appian serves a clear and specific dramatic function, but it is Plutarch's *Life of Antony* which was his primary classical source, as indeed it had been Shakespeare's. It is from Plutarch that Dryden derives the narrative line into which he introduces the type of detail from Appian and Dio which has been instanced above. Dryden also maintains many of Plutarch's narrative details, of which some, for example the description of the death tableau with which the play ends, had also been used by Shakespeare, while others, such as Cleopatra's attack on Antony's marriage, and marriage in general, (II, 81–4) seem to have been introduced almost direct from Plutarch.

[2] Preface, ll. 14–15.

Such factors clearly suggest that Dryden relied extensively on the *Life of Antony*; a solitary verbal echo suggests that Dryden's use of this work may have been very detailed indeed: Ventidius describes Antony on becoming aware of his own misdeeds as 'full of sharp remorse' (I, 129), in what appears to be a direct translation of Plutarch's observation that 'when he did perceive his errors he showed keen repentance'.[3]

Whether Dryden was referring to the texts of Plutarch, Dio, and Appian or not, the reader is likely to be impressed by this studied use of his classical knowledge. The same care typifies his use of the dramatic sources to which the Preface also directs attention. Of these, it is inevitably Shakespeare who is the most influential. Obviously, Dryden draws most heavily on *Antony and Cleopatra*, from which he quotes, with varying degrees of adaptation, at any length up to that of the passage describing Cleopatra's progress along the Cydnos (*Antony and Cleopatra*, II. ii, 189–217; *All For Love*, III, 162–82), which has been widely taken as an index of the differences between Shakespeare's art and Dryden's. In many ways, however, it is more interesting to note the profusion and range of Dryden's references to other Shakespeare plays, presumably as part of the attempt to imitate Shakespeare's style to which he refers in the Preface. The fact that Dryden's observations about Shakespeare are nearly as often derogatory as they are eulogistic makes it difficult to suggest with any certainty what his motives for the adoption of such a style might have been. Certain points which consistently won Dryden's respect do, however, emerge. He admired Shakespeare's 'beauties and heights', his ability to write 'excellent scenes of passion', which could arouse both terror and pity, but particularly the former:[4] it is the ability to write elevatedly and emotively which Dryden seems to have admired most. In *Of Dramatic Poesy: an Essay*, Neander, who is generally taken as representing Dryden's views, says of Shakespeare

> ... he was the man who of all modern, and perhaps ancient poets, had the largest and most comprehensive soul. All the images of nature were still present to him, and he drew them not laboriously, but luckily: when he describes any thing, you more than see it, you feel it too.[5]

This passage may usefully be seen in conjunction with the point

---

[3] Plutarch, *Lives* with a translation by Bernadotte Perin (London: Loeb Classical Library, 1959), IX, 189.
[4] James Kinsley and George Parfitt, eds, *John Dryden: Selected Criticism* (Oxford, 1970), pp. 130, 137, 166.
[5] ibid., 56.

in Act I when Ventidius interrupts Antony's fantasies (adapted by
Dryden from *As You Like It*) to observe 'Methinks I fancy/Myself
there too'. (I, 240–1).

Dryden rightly points out in the Preface that there were many
plays about Antony and Cleopatra other than Shakespeare's. He
makes extensive use, mostly in Act V, of Samuel Daniel's *The
Tragedy of Cleopatra* (1594, revised 1607), a play written in imitation
of classical tragedy and dealing with the story of Cleopatra after
Antony's death. The most recent treatment of the theme was Sir
Charles Sedley's *Antony and Cleopatra*, which was first performed
ten months before *All For Love*, on 12 February 1677. Sedley
(1639–1701),[6] one of the Restoration wits, achieved some notoriety
for his riotous living shortly after 1660, but in middle age became a
respected Whig. His main literary talent lay in writing lyric poetry,
but he also wrote two comedies (*The Mulberry Garden*, 1668, and
*Bellamira*, 1687) and collaborated in a translation of Corneille's
*Pompée* (1663). *Antony and Cleopatra*, which he revised at the end
of his life under the title *Beauty the Conqueror* (1702), is a conventional rhymed neo-classical tragedy depicting the conflict within
Antony of the rival claims of his love for Cleopatra and his honour,
against a background not only of the war being waged against
Octavius, but also of the plots and counter-plots of two noble but
misguided Egyptians, Memnon and Chilax, and of Photinus, whose
machinations almost swamp the rest of the action in the play.
This emphasis on the political context of the events points to an
intention on Sedley's part of criticizing Charles II by drawing
analogies between his way of life and that of Antony, whose overriding passion for Cleopatra leads to tyrannical misgovernment. The
tradition, dating back to the early years of the eighteenth century,
that Sedley gave Dryden the idea for his play[7] gains credibility from
their having in common features which cannot be explained by the
fact that both playwrights were writing within broadly similar
dramatic conventions. Of the plays about Antony's and Cleopatra's
deaths, only Dryden's and Sedley's have an identical timespan,
from the aftermath of the battle of Actium to Cleopatra's death. In
Sedley's play Dryden could have found, in somewhat embryonic
form, the use of contrasting imagery for the rival worlds of Egypt
(warm, sensuous, and erotic) and Rome (cold, militaristic, and

---

[6] See Vivian de Sola Pinto, *Sir Charles Sedley* (London, 1927).

[7] Vivian de Sola Pinto (ibid., p. 279) quotes from a poem by Eusden:
   So Dryden sweetest sang by envy fired;
   Thirst of revenge, when Phoebus failed, inspired:
   His Antony did Sedley's muse o'ertake, . . .

intellectual).[8] More important, Dryden adapts Sedley's scheme for giving Cleopatra an unambiguous tragic stature at the end of the play by placing the responsibility for the false news of her death on another character.

An attempt to follow the entire development of Alexas, the character used by Dryden for this purpose, provides the clearest indication of the complexity of his source material and the way in which he worked with it. In Plutarch, Alexas is a luxury-loving Greek; there are passing references to a Mardian; Cleopatra sends news of her supposed death by an unnamed messenger. Shakespeare makes Alexas a more important figure, and creates on the basis of the hint mentioned above, the character of Mardian, the eunuch whom Cleopatra instructs to tell Antony of her death. Sedley makes use of neither Alexas nor Mardian, but introduces instead the character of Photinus, who, according to Plutarch, was an Egyptian eunuch who plotted against Julius Caesar and Cleopatra. Shakespeare's Mardian may have influenced Sedley, but his primary sources appear to have been Fletcher's *The False One*, which Sedley may have known, and Corneille's *Pompée*, which he had helped to translate in about 1663. Sedley's Photinus, his virility restored, spends the entire play plotting the downfall of Antony and Cleopatra: his announcement of Cleopatra's death to Antony, to precipitate Antony's suicide, is his final manoeuvre in his secret attempts to form an alliance with Octavius. Given the political tone of the play, this would seem to be an attack on Danby, Charles II's chief minister, and the person to whom the Epistle Dedicatory to *All For Love* is addressed: the articles of impeachment drawn up against him in 1678 included charges that he had carried on secret negotiations with a foreign power, and had tried to introduce 'an arbitrary and tyrannical way of government'.[9] Dryden appears to fuse the roles of Shakespeare's Alexas and Mardian, and combine with this certain aspects of Photinus's role: while not as dangerous politically, Alexas's machinations are reminiscent of Photinus's, particularly in the case of his invention of

[8] See, for instance, Sedley's *Antony and Cleopatra*, III.ii, 75–81.

> CLEOPATRA
>> Sure of this war I am the mere pretence:
>> How can our love to Rome give such offence?
>> She should revenge the ghost of Crassus slain,
>> And haughty Babel level with the plain,
>> But let in Egypt love and pleasure reign.
>
> ANTONY
>> Rome, like her eagles, did on rapine thrive;
>> I am the first that taught her how to give.

Vivian de Sola Pinto, ed., *The Poetical and Dramatic Works of Sir Charles Sedley* (London, 1928), II, 220.

[9] A. Browning, ed., *English Historical Documents* (London, 1953), VIII, 198.

the news of Cleopatra's death out of sheer expediency. Dryden takes the credit for making Alexas a powerful symbol of the ultimate inadequacy, impotence, and self-interest of pure Reason, much vaunted at the time as the 'godlike' faculty in man, and responsible, among other things, for the narrow-mindedness of orthodox neo-classical literary theory.

In view of the almost scholarly way in which Dryden appears to have approached his sources, it is ironical that Neander's praise of Shakespeare quoted above continues:

> Those who accuse him to have wanted learning, give him the greater commendation: he was naturally learn'd; he needed not the spectacles of books to read Nature; he looked inwards, and found her there.[10]

## THE PLAY

A comparison of Sedley's *Antony and Cleopatra* and Dryden's *All For Love* highlights crucial aspects of the latter which may otherwise pass unnoticed. Certainly the points which Sedley's and Dryden's plays have in common suggest that Dryden not only found a source of dramatic ideas in Sedley's play, but also intended his own work to be seen in direct relationship to it. Such a conjecture is substantiated to a considerable extent by references in the Preface, in which Dryden not only implies the identity of the object of his attention, but also begins to define the form which he wants the relationship with it to take. It is a commonplace to note that in the Preface Dryden satirizes the earl of Rochester in revenge for the latter's attack on him in his poem *An Allusion to Horace*. While this accounts for many of the references in the Preface, Rochester cannot be taken as the sole butt for Dryden's derogatory remarks unless it is assumed that Dryden's satirical aim was unusually poor on this occasion. At the time when Rochester's lyrics were mostly cynical to say the least, and when the most controversial of his output consisted of the satires on which his present reputation largely stands, calling him a 'little sonneteer'[11] would hardly seem appropriate. Nor would jibes at wits who misapplied their talents to the writing of tragedies, or at critics who derive their criteria from the French, seem any nearer to the mark:[12] Rochester's adaptation of Fletcher's *Valentinian* appeared after *All For Love*, and certainly his attack on Dryden in *An Allusion to Horace* is not based on any critical theory which can be extrapolated; indeed, he makes the point

[10] Kinsley and Parfitt, op. cit., p. 56.
[11] Preface, l. 119.
[12] ibid., ll. 142, 115.

that Dryden shows too little respect for Shakespeare, Jonson, and Fletcher. It seems much more likely that Dryden is drawing attention to the fact that he is attacking not only Rochester but also Sedley, a poet whose reputation does stand on his songs, a wit who had turned his hand rather unsuccessfully to tragedy, and a critic whose preference for French drama had, according to tradition, been recorded by Dryden himself in the form of Lisideius's speeches in *Of Dramatic Poesy*.[13]

Clearly the amount of space which Dryden affords in the Preface to deriding French dramatic practice is greater than would be justified purely by personal animosity towards Sedley. It seems reasonable to suppose rather that Dryden was motivated by his desire to refute Sedley's attack on Charles II by not only discrediting him personally but also calling into question the validity of some of the dramatic conventions within which he was writing. The broader political significance is quite clear. Although neo-classicism was not unknown before 1660, it was in the years following the Restoration that it achieved its greatest currency. This was certainly in part due to its political implications, which may conveniently be illustrated by reference to Thomas Hobbes, whose aesthetic theory, the corollary of his political theory of autocratic totalitarianism expounded in *Leviathan* (1651), was identical in most respects to that of the French critics. Their ideas, while very differently derived, also formed part of an absolute monarchical system, that of Louis XIV,

[13] In particular there is evidence that Dryden's comments in the Preface were taken as an attack on Sedley, at least by Shadwell. The latter dedicated his comedy *A True Widow* to Sedley, and, in the Epistle Dedicatory (dated 16 February 1679) he wrote: '. . . in *Antony and Cleopatra* [you have shown] the true spirit of a tragedy, the only one (except two of Jonson's and one of Shakespeare's) wherein Romans are made to speak and do like Romans: there are to be found the true characters of Antony and Cleopatra as they were; whereas a French author would have made the Egyptian and the Roman both become French under his pen. And even our English authors are too much given to make true history in their plays romantic and impossible; but in this play, the Romans are true Romans and their style is such: and I dare affirm that there is not in any play of this age so much of the spirit of the classic authors, as in your *Antony and Cleopatra*' (Montague Summers, ed., *The Complete Works of Thomas Shadwell* (London, 1927), III, 283–4). Shadwell, who was, like Sedley, subsequently a Whig, was clearly defending Sedley against Dryden's attack, by emphasizing Sedley's classicism rather than his French neo-classicism. The terms 'romantic and impossible' are clearly an attack on *All For Love*.

The relationship which this implies between Shadwell and Dryden, who wrote a Prologue to *A True Widow*, seems rather complicated, but may perhaps be clarified by the fact that if play and prologue were ready for production by March 1678, but the play was not published until 1679, the manuscript version of *MacFlecknoe* probably appeared in the meantime.

whose power was the object amongst the English of a fear which was
to erupt into hysterical hatred of the French and persecution of
Catholics after Titus Oates's revelation of the supposed Popish Plot
in 1678. Hobbes wrote in the Preface to his translation of the *Odyssey*
(1675):

> The virtues required of an heroic poem, and indeed in all writings
> published, are comprehended all in this one word: discretion. And
> discretion consisteth in this, that every part of the poem be con-
> ducing, and in good order placed, to the end and design of the poet.
> And the design is not only to profit, but also to delight the reader.
> By profit I intend not here any accession of wealth, either to the
> poet or to the reader, but accession of prudence, justice, fortitude,
> by the example of such great and noble persons as he introduceth
> speaking or describeth acting.[14]

Overt didacticism is thus a fundamental feature of conventional
neo-classical drama: the fact that the examples offered for imitation
are all of 'great and noble persons' implies a conservative élitism
which Hobbes had made more explicit in his answer to Davenant's
Preface to *Gondibert* (1650):

> As philosophers have divided the universe, their subject, into
> three regions, celestial, aerial, and terrestrial, so the poets, whose
> work it is, by imitating human life in delightful and measured lines,
> to avert men from vice and incline them to virtuous and honourable
> actions, have lodged themselves in the three regions of mankind,
> court, city, and country, correspondent in some proportion to those
> three regions of the world. For there is in princes and men of
> conspicuous power, anciently called heroes, a lustre and influence
> upon the rest of men resembling that of the Heavens; and an
> insincereness, inconstancy, and troublesome humour of those that
> dwell in populous cities, like the mobility, blustering, and impurity
> of the air; and a plainness, and though dull, yet a nutritive faculty
> in rural people that endures a comparison with the earth they
> labour. From hence have proceeded three sorts of poetry, heroic,
> scommatic, and pastoral ... the heroic poem narrative ... is called
> an epic poem. The heroic poem dramatic is tragedy.[15]

In England, the plays which observed such dictates had strong
jingoistic overtones, their emphasis on the superhuman nobility of
an aristocratic or royal élite being used less as an example to others
than as a vehicle for a panegyric on the newly restored monarch. The
central conflict of the typical heroic play was one between love and

[14] J. E. Spingarn, ed., *Critical Essays of the Seventeenth Century* (Bloomington
and London, 1957), II, 67–8.
[15] ibid., 54–5.

honour. While *All For Love* clearly illustrates the strengths and appeal of the portrayal of such a situation, it gave rise to many tendentious stereotyped works which, as early as 1671, the duke of Buckingham had burlesqued in *The Rehearsal*:

VOLSCIUS *sits down to pull on his boots* . . .

VOLSCIUS
How has my passion made me Cupid's scoff!
This hasty boot is on, the other off,
And sullen lies, with amorous design
To quit loud fame, and make that beauty mine . . .
My legs, the emblem of my various thought,
Show to what sad distraction I am brought.
Sometimes with stubborn Honour, like this boot,
My mind is guarded, and resolved to do't:
Sometimes again, that very mind, by Love
Disarmed, like this other leg does prove.
Shall I to Honour or to Love give way?
'Go on', cries Honour; tender Love says 'Nay'.
Honour aloud commands 'Pluck both boots on',
But softer Love does whisper 'Put on none'.
What shall I do? What conduct shall I find
To lead me through this twilight of my mind?
For, as bright day with black approach of night
Contending makes a doubtful puzzling light,
So does my Honour and my Love together
Puzzle me so, I can resolve for neither.
*Goes out hopping, with one boot on and the other off* [16]

The conventional subordination of the selfish interests of love to the altruistic demands of honour underlined the individual's duty to the state and the evils of rebellion. Sedley used such criteria to show how far short of the heroic ideal Charles II's pursuit of self-gratification had made him fall: Sedley even goes as far as portraying the motives of the Egyptian rebels Chilax and Memnon as understandable if inexcusable.

In replying to Sedley's play, Dryden chose not to write an orthodox eulogy on Charles's virtually non-existent high-mindedness, but rather to undermine the criteria on which Sedley's attack was based. He attempts to arouse patriotic feelings in the Preface by celebrating the supremacy of English drama as exemplified by 'the divine Shakespeare', building on growing anti-French feeling in order to make French dramatists, and Racine in particular, suffer cruelly by comparison; it is worth noting that the play which Dryden chooses to ridicule is *Phèdre*, which was published only eight months

[16] Simon Trussler, ed., *Burlesque Plays of the Eighteenth Century* (London, 1969), pp. 33–4.

before *All For Love* appeared on the Stationers' Register: presumably Dryden's intention was to capitalize on the stir which one may imagine the recent arrival of the play would have created in Francophile circles:

> ... their Hippolytus is so scrupulous in point of decency that he will rather expose himself to death than accuse his stepmother to his father, and my critics, I am sure, will commend him for it; but we of grosser apprehensions are apt to think that this excess of generosity is not practicable but with fools and madmen.
>
> (ll. 94–99)

The idea of practicability is quiet alien to neo-classical theory, with its emphasis on the ideal rather than the viable. Clearly, if Dryden can substantiate this point, Sedley's play is to a considerable extent invalidated. Immediately after this attack on the moral narrow-mindedness of French critics, he goes on to say: 'Our little sonneteers who follow them have too narrow souls to judge of poetry'. The intrusion of the word 'soul' is important: poetry is something, he implies, which transcends conventional moral considerations in its search for spiritual fulfilment. The idea behind this image recurs in Ventidius's description of Antony:

> Virtue's his path; but sometimes 'tis too narrow
> For his vast soul, and then he starts out wide
> And bounds into a vice that bears him far
> From his first course, and plunges him in ills ...
>
> (I, 124–7)

The image is a bold one, and quite probably 'morally ... unsound', as Kenneth Muir states.[17] Nonetheless, it is apparent that, when seen in relation to the comment in the Preface, and to Dryden's two references to the 'largeness' of Shakespeare's soul, it constitutes one of the cruces of Dryden's argument. Vastness of the soul is clearly a rendering into English of *Magnanimitas*, a word implying high-mindedness, courage, and all regal qualities. The obvious translation would have been 'great soul', and the fact that Dryden chooses an adjective other than the obvious one is significant: not only does it underline the physicality on which the effect of the image relies, but also it may suggest not simply the Latin source of the term, but the Greek one, *Megalopsychia*, which is defined by Aristotle in the *Nicomachean Ethics*:

[17] Kenneth Muir, 'The Imagery of *All For Love*', in Bruce King, ed., *Twentieth Century Interpretations of All For Love* (Englewood Cliffs, N.J., 1968), p. 33.

Greatness of Soul, as the word itself implies, seems to be related to great objects ... a person is thought to be great-souled if he claims much and deserves much ... He who deserves little and claims little is modest or temperate, but not great-souled, since to be great-souled involves greatness, just as handsomeness involves size ... Though therefore in regard to the greatness of his claim the great-souled man is an extreme, by reason of its rightness he stands at the mean point, for he claims what he deserves; while the vain and the small-souled err by excess and defect respectively. If then the great-souled man claims and is worthy of great things and most of all the greatest things, Greatness of Soul must be concerned with some one object especially ... Now the greatest ... good we should assume to be the thing which we offer as a tribute to the gods, and which is most coveted by men of high station, and is the prize awarded for the noblest deeds; and such a thing is honour ... And inasmuch as the great-souled man deserves most, he must be the best of men ... Great honours accorded by persons of worth will afford him pleasure in a moderate degree ... Honour rendered by common people and on trivial grounds he will utterly despise.[18]

This philosophical attitude appears in particular to underlie Antony's relationship with Octavia. Antony himself refers to her 'greatness of soul' (III, 314) in the course of a scene in which it emerges that, at least in the Aristotelian sense, she has no such thing. She claims Antony ('Your hand, my Lord; 'tis mine, and I will have it'; III, 266), but makes it clear that this claim is not for 'one object especially', but a proposal made for a variety of reasons, marital, maternal, and political, which makes her ready to compromise even to the extent of yielding up any claim to him:

I'll tell my brother we are reconciled;
He shall draw back his troops, and you shall march
To rule the East: I may be dropped at Athens—
No matter where, I never will complain,
But only keep the barren name of wife,
And rid you of the trouble.                          (III, 300–305)

Her attitude is clearly 'modest or temperate' rather than great-souled. Dryden has found a context in which the conventional reactions to the appeals of honour associated with marital obligations and patriotic duty can be depicted as resulting from an inadequate response to Antony's situation; what he, as a great-souled hero, deserves is the only object of greatness untrammelled by other considerations, Cleopatra's love, and since this is what he deserves, his remaining with Cleopatra is ultimately the most honourable course to pursue, even though it seems dishonourable to 'common

[18] Aristotle, *Nichomachean Ethics*, with a translation by H. Rackham (London: Loeb Classical Library, 1968), pp. 213–19.

people'. Dryden's argument has in a sense gone full circle: in attacking the élitist assumption that heroes lead exemplary lives, an essential point to neo-classical literary theory (which was, or thought itself to be, derived originally from Aristotle's *Poetics*), he appeals to a theory of identical authority which is still more select, because it defies not only imitation, but also judgement by lesser mortals. Sedley had written in his Prologue:

> Cripples may judge of vaulting, he well knows,
> Cowards of courage, and of verse and prose
> They that know neither . . . [19]

Dryden, having established the Aristotelian context for his theory, contradicts this democratic notion (Preface, ll. 128–46):

> . . . the crowd cannot be presumed to have more than a gross instinct of what pleases or displeases them . . . But . . . I come closer to those who are allowed for witty men, either by the advantage of their quality or by common fame, and affirm that neither are they qualified to decide sovereignly concerning poetry . . . there are many witty men, but few poets; neither have all poets a taste of tragedy. And this is the rock on which they are daily splitting. Poetry, which is a picture of nature, must generally please; but 'tis not to be understood that all parts of it must please every man.

While Dryden is clearly staying within the bounds of neo-classical theory, one should not underestimate the extent to which he is breaking with heroic convention, to which the idea that the world could be well lost for love would be wholly alien. Thus Dr Johnson, writing a hundred years later, said of the play:

> It is by universal consent accounted the work in which he has admitted the fewest improprieties of style or character; but it has one fault equal to many, though rather moral than critical, that by admitting the romantic omnipotence of love, he has recommended as laudable and worthy of imitation that conduct which through all ages the good have censured as vicious and the bad despised as foolish.[20]

This is strongly reminiscent of Johnson's criticism of Pope's *Elegy to the Memory of an Unfortunate Lady*, with which Dryden's play had several affinities, though none of them close enough to suggest that Pope was actually indebted to Dryden. While I think it would be mistaken to go as far as the *Penguin Book of Romantic Verse*, the first poem in which is Pope's *Elegy*, it is certain that Dryden is providing a very early example of the sentimentalism which was to develop into one aspect of Romanticism.

[19] Pinto, *The Poetical and Dramatic Works of Sir Charles Sedley*, II, 191.
[20] Samuel Johnson, *Lives of English Poets* (London, 1904, reprint 1952), I, 256–7.

Dryden's attitude does, however, differ radically from proto-romantic sentimentalism in a manner which goes some way towards invalidating criticisms such as Johnson's. Antony says in the scene between him and Octavia: '... I can ne'er be conquered but by love,/And you do all for duty'. (III, 316–17). Cleopatra's love for Antony is certainly described in absolute terms which suggest 'the romantic omnipotence of love':

> My love's a noble madness,
> Which shows the cause deserved it. Moderate sorrow
> Fits vulgar love, and for a vulgar man;
> But I have loved with such transcendent passion,
> I soared at first quite out of reason's view,
> And now am lost above it.                (II, 17–22)

The Aristotelian notion of greatness of soul and its immunity to adverse criticism is implied here, but Dryden also suggests another frame of reference within which he will attempt to define rather than simply assert the value and power of love. Both reason and honour are apparently opposed to this love. The worth of pure reason as a basis for action is totally undermined by Dryden's identification of it with the petty self-interested and ultimately destructive attitudes and plans of Alexas, who by virtue of his emasculation 'bears his reason undisturbed'. Thus far Dryden proceeds without difficulty: there remains, however, the problem of demonstrating that Cleopatra's love is the highest, and the most honourable, thing to which Antony can aspire. When Antony describes to Cleopatra the dishonourable acts which his love has led him to commit, he starts by saying:

> If I mix a lie
> With any truth, reproach me freely with it;
> Else favour me with silence.                (II, 253–5)

This is a clear reference to Plato's *Symposium*, in which Alcibiades, another hero who was the subject of one of Plutarch's *Lives*, starts his description of his love for Socrates, and Socrates' love for him, by saying: 'if I say anything which is not true, you may interrupt me if you will, and say "that is a lie"'. Alcibiades continues:

> ... if I did not shut my ears against him, and fly as from the ...
> siren, I could not hold out against him, and my fate would be like
> that of others,—he would pin me down, and I should grow old
> sitting at his feet. For he makes me confess that I ought not to live
> as I do, neglecting the many wants of my own soul and busying
> myself with the concerns of the Athenians.[21]

[21] B. Jowett, trans., *Dialogues of Plato* (4th edition, Oxford, 1953), I, 547–8. Given the Platonic context which this reference implies, it appears likely that Cleopatra's 'noble madness' (II, 17) owes something to Plato's *Phaedrus*.

Antony, then, it is implied, should be turning his attention to the wants of his own soul. Yet he already has a love, Dollabella, who is clearly in the Platonic mould. Dollabella is his 'better half' (III, 119), and their relationship made them 'one mass' (III, 96): in the *Symposium* Aristophanes explains precisely such a relationship by a fantastic account of how humans were originally joined together, but having been divided, spend their lives searching for their other half, united with whom they are whole, and from whom they cannot again be divided. Such a friendship would have been entirely compatible with the tenets of neo-classical criticism; Dryden himself wrote:

> Friendship is both a virtue and a passion essentially; love is a passion only in its nature, and is not a virtue but by accident: good nature makes friendship, but effeminacy love.[22]

Yet, just as Reason in the shape of Alexas falls short of the claims made for it by its proponents, so Dollabella's pure and virtuous friendship with Antony can be corrupted and destroyed by his passion for Cleopatra: not only does he woo her for himself, but he also lies poisonously about Antony.

So, finally, one comes to the love of Antony and Cleopatra, which by Platonic convention must be inferior to love between men. Yet it is in terms derived from Plato that Dryden seeks ultimately to validate Cleopatra's love. The *Symposium* describes three ascending levels of love: the first, physical and romantic, for one person alone; the second intellectual and for more than one person; and the last spiritual, for an object of absolute divine value. The lover's aim should be to reach this ultimate plane. These three levels of being lie behind the physiological system mentioned by Dryden in the Epistle Dedicatory (ll. 73–78) and are referred to specifically by Hobbes in his account of the three realms of literary activity. Cleopatra refers to the status of a wife on three occasions which should be juxtaposed to such a doctrine. She first describes a wife as 'That dull, insipid lump, without desires,/And without power to give 'em . . .' (III, 83–4): dullness is an adjective used by Hobbes to describe the lowest state of life, which physiologically would be identified with the insensate vegetal element of man. In Act IV, after Antony's rejection of her, Cleopatra says:

> Nature meant me
> A wife, a silly, harmless, household dove,
> Fond without art, and kind without deceit . . .                    (91–3)

[22] Kinsley and Parfitt, op. cit., p. 177.

The dove, obviously, is a creature of Hobbes's aerial realm; equally, the domestic setting evoked is of the bourgeois world from which Hobbes's scommatic literature takes its subject-matter.

When planning her own death at the end of the play, Cleopatra's attitude to the role of a wife is finally compatible with her description of her love for Antony in Act II:

I have not loved a Roman not to know
What should become his wife—his wife, my Charmion,
For 'tis to that high title I aspire,
And now I'll not die less. Let dull Octavia
Survive to mourn him dead; my nobler fate
Shall knit our spousals with a tie too strong
For Roman laws to break.                    (V, 412–18)

Dryden appears to apply a double standard here: an appeal to the patriotic aspect of honour is made at the start of a speech which concludes by belittling its source. Cleopatra's love is to be seen in the context of divine rather than human laws. Her ascent to Hobbes's sphere of celestial lustre is complete, and, unconditionally and uncompromisingly, she 'arrives at ... the science which has no other object but absolute beauty, and at last knows that which is beautiful alone'.[23] Her love is in Platonic terms of a divine nature, and thus satisfies Aristotle's requirement that the object of a great-souled hero's desires must be 'what we offer as a tribute to the gods'. The denial of the claims of family, country, honour, and ultimately of life itself is portrayed as necessary to this apotheosis, symbolized by the final tableau of Antony and Cleopatra in death, enthroned in unassailable regal splendour.

This, at least, appears to be Dryden's intention in the play. In fact, however, there may be cause to doubt whether he does attain such grandiose objectives, or whether, beneath the controlled brilliance of his argument and his rather ostentatious display of erudition, there remains a gap between intention and achievement: the reader may feel that, behind the verbiage, Dryden's argument is not tight enough to convince him that Antony and Cleopatra's relationship is of such a lofty philosophical order. The sheer intellectual power demonstrated in the play certainly justifies the most serious critical attention, but if these comments are accepted, they must qualify any assessment of the play to a considerable extent. Nevertheless, *All For Love* has retained not only the respect of the critics, but also the interest of theatre audiences, whose attraction to the play can only be explained by recognizing that it manifests some essentially dramatic aspects of Dryden's genius.

Perhaps the most obvious facet of the play's theatrical qualities

[23] Jowett, ed. cit., 543.

is the sense of movement which is evident in it: here, comparison
with Shakespeare may be constructive. Dryden has pared down
*dramatis personae* and action to essentials; the stage is occupied for
the most part by few characters, each of whom has a clearly defined
position and role. The play progresses to its denouement through a
series of shifting patterns, clearly exemplified by the part played by
Ventidius: in Act I he raises Antony from despondency by appealing
to his sense of honour: in Act II he is rebuffed by Antony as Cleopatra arouses his love; in Act III his influence is once again dominant
as he engineers the encounter between Antony and Octavia; in Act
IV this influence, while still overriding, is shown to be hollow, his
simple dignity and straightforward honour undermined by his
desire to defeat Cleopatra at all costs; in Act V his sense of honour
is, in death, finally reconciled with Antony's. Such a pattern, in
which Ventidius's fortunes rise and fall as Antony swings first
towards the appeal of honour and then towards that of love, is
typical of many neo-classical tragedies. While not unattractive, this
schema, like Ventidius's character, is static. It gains a dynamic
strength, however, from the introduction into this conventional
form of a variety of other patterns of movement: a romantic and
sentimental climax in Act III, as Antony first celebrates his love
for Cleopatra and then turns his back on it when confronted by the
claims of a friend, wife, and children; a pathetic climax in Act IV, as
Antony and Cleopatra face what appears to be total ruin of their lives;
and finally, the tragic climax of Act V, towards which the entire
action tends, and of which the other patterns are subordinate parts.

Recognition of the theatrical purity and structural beauty of *All
For Love* accounts for some of its appeal, but not for its power to
arouse strong emotional reactions even on a casual reading. What
was referred to earlier as the 'tendentious stereotype' which many
Restoration dramatists seem to have felt constrained to produce by
the conventions of the time tends to fall into an emotional frigidity
which the modern audience is likely to be out of sympathy with. It
does not follow from this, however, that within the convention of
the conflict of love and honour there are not perceptions of human
behaviour, which Dryden and a small number of his contemporaries
recognized. That such perceptions do inform the action of *All For
Love* with a real emotional power emerges most forcibly in two
scenes which have superficial similarities but totally different tones.
In Act II Antony, apparently confident in his reawoken sense of
honour, chooses to confront Cleopatra rather than leave without
seeing her. To Ventidius's objections he replies 'I'm constant to
myself, I know my strength; . . .' (II, 229). His assessment of what
Cleopatra's love has cost (II, 262–321) certainly indicates a degree
of critical lucidity which only his uncompromising intention of

leaving honourably could make possible. Yet he does not go: he is compelled, by his very constancy to himself, by his own judgement of values, to place himself in a position in which he will, as Ventidius knows, be dissuaded from going, and rather to stay on a revitalized basis of the mutual honesty which his attempt to leave has resulted in. The reader will here recognize some psychological truth: this is the way that people behave.

At the end of Act IV, Antony again intends to part from Cleopatra, and again confronts her with this intention. In this case, Dryden captures not so much a perception of how people act as a mood, one of total pathos. Antony's bitter anger at the ruinous deceptions he has been acutely vulnerable to and the almost masochistic delight he takes in denouncing Dollabella and Cleopatra give way to a final dejected admission of the emptiness which they and their circumstances have produced. Genuine and powerful emotions are involved in the play, and, whatever its philosophical flaws, this does give it dignity and stature: if the play does ultimately fail, it is a glorious failure.

## NOTES ON THE TEXT

The first edition of *All For Love* was the quarto printed by Thomas Newcomb for Henry Herringman. According to the entry in the Stationers' Register, it was licensed by Sir Roger l'Estrange, licenser of the press, on 31 January 1678, and the evidence of an advertisement in *The London Gazette* suggests that it appeared in late March that year. The first quarto (Q1) is the only authoritative text, and the Scolar Press facsimile of this quarto has been used as the copy text for this edition. Spelling has been modernized throughout, as it has been when a quotation has been made from any work using original spelling. Eleven corrections to the text were made during printing (of which four are recorded in this edition), and it is from a copy of Q1 containing all the corrected readings that the second quarto (Q2) was printed, again for Henry Herringman, in 1692. The third quarto (Q3) of 1696 was printed from a copy of the second quarto, and the first collected edition of the dramatic works (W1), two folio volumes published in 1701, in turn followed Q3. This history goes to provide a typical example of progressive textual corruption, which Congreve and Tonson, the editors of the 1717 six-volume *Dramatic Works* (W2), attempted to remedy by using a copy of Q1, in which some of the uncorrected readings were evidently present.[24]

[24] See Hugh Macdonald, *John Dryden: A Bibliography of Early Editions and Drydeniana* (Oxford, 1939) for bibliographical descriptions and details.

## ABBREVIATIONS

| | |
|---|---|
| ed. | editor |
| *ELH* | *English Literary History* |
| *N & Q* | *Notes and Queries* |
| om. | omits |
| *Poems* | *The Poems of John Dryden*, ed. James Kinsley (Oxford, 1958) |
| Q1 | First quarto of 1678 |
| Q2 | Second quarto of 1692 |
| Q3 | Third quarto of 1696 |
| s.d. | stage direction |
| W1 | Collected edition of dramatic works, 1701 |
| W2 | 6-volume *Dramatic Works* of 1717 |

## FURTHER READING

Robert D. Hume, *The Development of English Drama in the Late Seventeenth Century* (Oxford, 1976).

Derek W. Hughes, 'The Significance of *All For Love*', *ELH* 37 (1970), 540–63.

D. W. Jefferson, 'The Significance of Dryden's Heroic Plays' in *Restoration Dramatists*, ed. Earl Miner (Englewood Cliffs, N.J., 1966), pp. 19–35.

R. J. Kaufmann, 'On the Poetics of Terminal Tragedy: Dryden's *All For Love*' in *Dryden*, ed. Bernard Schilling (Englewood Cliffs, N.J., 1963), pp. 86–94.

Bruce King, ed., *Twentieth Century Interpretations of All For Love* (Englewood Cliffs, N.J., 1968).

Eric Rothstein, *Restoration Tragedy* (Madison, Milwaukee/London, 1967).

Eugene M. Waith, '*All For Love*' in *Restoration Dramatists*, ed. Earl Miner, pp. 51–62.

# ALL FOR LOVE:

## OR, THE

# World well Loſt.

## A

# TRAGEDY,

As it is Acted at the

## *THEATRE-ROYAL;*

And Written in Imitation of *Shakeſpeare's* Stile.

By *John Dryden*, Servant to His Majeſty.

*Facile eſt verbum aliquod ardens (ut ita dicam) notare : idque re-
ſtinctis animorum incendiis irridere.* Cicero.

*In the SAVOY:*

Printed by *Tho. Newcomb*, for *Henry Herringman*, at the Blew An-
chor in the Lower Walk of the *New-Exchange.* 1678.

---

Facile est ... irridere Cicero, *Orator* viii, 27. Dryden omits the word
'enim' after 'est', and 'iam' after 'restinctis'. 'It is easy [indeed] to
criticize some flaming word (if I may use the expression) and to laugh at
it when the passion [of the moment] has cooled'. Cicero, *Brutus and
Orator*, with a translation by G. L. Hendrickson and H. M. Hubbell
(London: Loeb Classical Library, 1939), p. 323.

## EPISTLE DEDICATORY

To the Right Honourable Thomas, Earl of Danby, Viscount
Latimer, and Baron Osborne of Kiveton in Yorkshire, Lord
High Treasurer of England, One of His Majesty's Most
Honourable Privy Council, and Knight of the Most Noble
Order of the Garter, etc.                                                  5

My Lord,

   The gratitude of poets is so troublesome a virtue to great
men that you are often in danger of your own benefits, for
you are threatened with some epistle, and not suffered to do
good in quiet, or to compound for their silence whom you    10
have obliged. Yet, I confess, I neither am nor ought to be
surprised at this indulgence, for your Lordship has the same
right to favour poetry which the great and noble have ever
had:

   *Carmen amat, quisquis carmine digna gerit.*                15

   There is somewhat of a tie in nature betwixt those who are
born for worthy actions and those who can transmit them to
posterity, and though ours be much the inferior part, it
comes at least within the verge of alliance; nor are we un-
profitable members of the commonwealth, when we animate    20
others to those virtues which we copy and describe from you.

   'Tis indeed their interest who endeavour the subversion of
governments to discourage poets and historians, for the best
which can happen to them is to be forgotten: but such who,
under kings, are the fathers of their country, and by a just    25

---

1 *Danby* Thomas Osborne (1631–1712; created earl of Danby in 1674)
became Lord High Treasurer and Charles II's chief minister in 1673.
In 1675 an unsuccessful attempt to impeach him on charges of bribery
was made; in December 1678, he was impeached, and, despite some
protection from Charles II, he was imprisoned in the Tower until 1684.
His anti-Catholicism brought him into opposition during the reign of
James II, and after the revolution of 1688 he again held office during the
reign of William III and Mary II, becoming marquis of Carmarthen
and duke of Leeds. In 1695, his impeachment, this time on charges of
accepting bribes, marked the end of his political career.

15 *Carmen . . . gerit.* Claudian, Book III, Preface, 6, 'Whoever does deeds
worthy of poetry, loves poetry'. The passage is taken from a description
of how the elder Scipio took the poet Ennius on all his military cam-
paigns.

and prudent ordering of affairs preserve it, have the same
reason to cherish the chroniclers of their actions as they have
to lay up in safety the deeds and evidences of their estates,
for such records are their undoubted titles to the love and
reverence of after ages. Your Lordship's administration has          30
already taken up a considerable part of the English annals,
and many of its most happy years are owing to it. His Majesty,
the most knowing judge of men and the best master, has
acknowledged the ease and benefit he receives in the incomes
of his Treasury, which you found not only disordered but            35
exhausted. All things were in the confusion of a chaos,
without form or method, if not reduced beyond it even to
annihilation, so that you had not only to separate the jarring
elements, but (if that boldness of expression might be allowed
me) to create them. Your enemies had so embroiled the               40
management of your office that they looked on your advance-
ment as the instrument of your ruin. And, as if the clogging
of the revenue and the confusion of accounts which you
found in your entrance were not sufficient, they added their
own weight of malice to the public calamity by forestalling          45
the credit which should cure it. Your friends on the other
side were only capable of pitying, but not of aiding you. No
farther help or counsel was remaining to you but what was
founded on yourself, and that indeed was your security: for
your diligence, your constancy, and your prudence wrought            50
more surely within when they were not disturbed by any
outward motion. The highest virtue is best to be trusted with
itself, for assistance only can be given by a genius superior to
that which it assists. And 'tis the noblest kind of debt when
we are only obliged to God and Nature. This, then, my Lord,          55
is your just commendation, that you have wrought out yourself a way to glory by those very means that were designed for
your destruction. You have not only restored but advanced
the revenues of your master without grievance to the subject;
and as if that were little yet, the debts of the Exchequer,          60
which lay heaviest both on the Crown and on private persons,
have by your conduct been established in a certainty of
satisfaction: an action so much the more great and honourable because the case was without the ordinary relief of laws,
above the hopes of the afflicted, and beyond the narrowness          65
of the Treasury to redress, had it been managed by a less able
hand. 'Tis certainly the happiest and most unenvied part of
all your fortune to do good to many while you do injury to
none; to receive at once the prayers of the subject and the
praises of the prince; and by the care of your conduct, to give      70

him means of exerting the chiefest (if any be the chiefest) of
his royal virtues, his distributive justice to the deserving, and
his bounty and compassion to the wanting. The disposition
of princes towards their people cannot better be discovered
than in the choice of their ministers, who, like the animal      75
spirits betwixt the soul and body, participate somewhat of
both natures, and make the communication which is betwixt
them. A king who is just and moderate in his nature, who
rules according to the laws, whom God made happy by
forming the temper of his soul to the constitution of his        80
government, and who makes us happy by assuming over us
no other sovereignty than that wherein our welfare and
liberty consists: a prince, I say, of so excellent a character,
and so suitable to the wishes of all good men, could not better
have conveyed himself into his people's apprehensions than      85
in your Lordship's person, who so lively express the same
virtues that you seem not so much a copy as an emanation of
him. Moderation is doubtless an establishment of greatness,
but there is a steadiness of temper which is likewise requisite
in a minister of state: so equal a mixture of both virtues that  90
he may stand like an isthmus betwixt the two encroaching
seas of arbitrary power and lawless anarchy. The undertaking
would be difficult to any but an extraordinary genius, to
stand at the line and to divide the limits; to pay what is due
to the great representative of the nation, and neither to        95
enhance nor to yield up the undoubted prerogatives of the
Crown. These, my Lord, are the proper virtues of a noble
Englishman, as indeed they are properly English virtues, no
people in the world being capable of using them but we who
have the happiness to be born under so equal and so well-       100
poised a government: a government which has all the advantages of liberty beyond a commonwealth, and all the
marks of kingly sovereignty without the danger of a tyranny.
Both my nature, as I am an Englishman, and my reason,
as I am a man, have bred in me a loathing to that specious       105

---

75–6 *animal spirits* In the physiological system derived from the medical
  works of Galen, based on the platonic division of man into three parts,
  the body was capable only of the vegetal functions of nutrition and
  growth; the soul was responsible for feeling and motion; to explain how
  the soul, by definition incorporeal, could influence the physical behaviour of inanimate matter, the existence of animal spirits, distributed
  from the soul to various parts of the body by way of the arteries, was
  postulated.

name of a republic: that mock appearance of a liberty, where
all who have not part in the government are slaves, and slaves
they are of a viler note than such as are subjects to an absolute
dominion: for no Christian monarchy is so absolute but 'tis
circumscribed with laws; but when the executive power is in     110
the lawmakers, there is no farther check upon them, and the
people must suffer without a remedy because they are
oppressed by their representatives. If I must serve, the
number of my masters, who were born my equals, would but
add to the ignominy of my bondage. The nature of our        115
government, above all others, is exactly suited both to the
situation of our country and the temper of the natives, an
island being more proper for commerce and for defence than
for extending its dominions on the continent: for what the
valour of its inhabitants might gain, by reason of its remote-   120
ness and the casualties of the seas it could not so easily preserve; and therefore neither the arbitrary power of one in a
monarchy, nor of many in a commonwealth, could make us
greater than we are. 'Tis true that vaster and more frequent
taxes might be gathered when the consent of the people was    125
not asked or needed, but this were only by conquering
abroad to be poor at home; and the examples of our neighbours teach us that they are not always the happiest subjects
whose kings extend their dominions farthest. Since, therefore, we cannot win by an offensive war, at least a land war,    130
the model of our government seems naturally contrived for
the defensive part, and the consent of a people is easily ob-
tained to contribute to that power which must protect it.
*Felices nimium, bona si sua norint. Angligenae.* And yet there
are not wanting malcontents amongst us, who, surfeiting    135
themselves on too much happiness, would persuade the
people that they might be happier by a change. 'Twas indeed
the policy of their old forefather, when himself was fallen
from the station of glory, to seduce mankind into the same

---

127–8 *neighbours* Louis XIV's military conquests made the French the object
of fear.
134 *Felices . . . Angligenae* 'O happy Englishmen! Too happy, if they but
came to know it'. Adapted from Virgil, *Georgics*, II, 458–9, '*O fortunatos
nimium sua si bona norint,/Agricolas*'.
O happy, if he knew his happy state!
The swain, who, free from business and debate,
Receives his easy food from Nature's hand.
(Dryden's translation, ll. 639–41, *The Poems of John Dryden*, ed. James
Kinsley, Oxford, 1958, II, 953).

rebellion with him by telling him he might yet be freer than 140
he was: that is, more free than his nature would allow, or (if
I may so say) than God could make him. We have already all
the liberty which freeborn subjects can enjoy, and all beyond
it is but licence. But if it be liberty of conscience which they
pretend, the moderation of our church is such that its prac- 145
tice extends not to the severity of persecution, and its
discipline is withal so easy that it allows more freedom to
dissenters than any of the sects would allow to it. In the meantime, what right can be pretended by these men to attempt
innovations in church or state? Who made them the trustees 150
or (to speak a little nearer their own language) the keepers of
the liberty of England? If their call be extraordinary, let them
convince us by working miracles; for ordinary vocation they
can have none to disturb the government under which they
were born, and which protects them. He who has often 155
changed his party, and always has made his interest the rule
of it, gives little evidence of his sincerity for the public good:
'tis manifest he changes but for himself, and takes the people
for tools to work his fortune. Yet the experience of all ages
might let him know that they who trouble the waters first 160
have seldom the benefit of the fishing; as they who began the
late rebellion enjoyed not the fruit of their undertaking, but
were crushed themselves by the usurpation of their own
instrument. Neither is it enough for them to answer that
they only intend a reformation of the government, but not 165
the subversion of it: on such pretences all insurrections have
been founded; 'tis striking at the root of power, which is
obedience. Every remonstrance of private men has the seed
of treason in it, and discourses which are couched in am-
biguous terms are therefore the more dangerous because 170
they do all the mischief of open sedition, yet are safe from
the punishment of the laws. These, my Lord, are considerations which I should not pass so lightly over had I

170 *are* Q2, Q3, W1, W2 (ars Q1)

---

144 *liberty of conscience* Sir John Pollock lists sixteen penal laws, of which
   thirteen were directed specifically at Roman Catholics, which were on
   the statute books in 1678. *The Popish Plot* (Cambridge, 1903),
   pp. 400–4.
155–6 *He who has often changed his party* Anthony Ashley Cooper, first earl of
   Shaftesbury (1621–83), after frequent changes of political sides, was at
   the time in the process of forming what was to become the Whig party,
   and was thus Danby's chief political opponent. See also *Absalom and
   Achitophel* and *The Medal*.

room to manage them as they deserve; for no man can be so
inconsiderable in a nation as not to have a share in the welfare   175
of it, and, if he be a true Englishman, he must at the same
time be fired with indignation, and revenge himself as he can
on the disturbers of his country. And to whom could I more
fitly apply myself than to your Lordship, who have not only
an inborn but an hereditary loyalty? The memorable con-   180
stancy and sufferings of your father, almost to the ruin of his
estate for the royal cause, were an earnest of that which such
a parent and such an institution would produce in the person
of a son. But so unhappy an occasion of manifesting your
own zeal in suffering for his present Majesty, the Providence   185
of God and the prudence of your administration will, I hope,
prevent; that as your father's fortune waited on the un-
happiness of his sovereign, so your own may participate of
the better fate which attends his son. The relation which you
have by alliance to the noble family of your lady serves to   190
confirm to you both this happy augury. For what can deserve
a greater place in the English chronicle than the loyalty and
courage, the actions and death, of the general of an army
fighting for his prince and country? The honour and gallantry
of the Earl of Lindsey is so illustrious a subject that 'tis fit   195
to adorn an heroic poem, for he was the proto-martyr of the
cause, and the type of his unfortunate royal master.

Yet, after all, my Lord, if I may speak my thoughts, you
are happy rather to us than to yourself: for the multiplicity,
the cares, and the vexations of your employment have be-   200
trayed you from yourself, and given you up into the possession of the public. You are robbed of your privacy and
friends, and scarce any hour of your life you can call your
own. Those who envy your fortune, if they wanted not good
nature, might more justly pity it; and when they see you   205
watched by a crowd of suitors, whose importunity 'tis impossible to avoid, would conclude with reason that you have
lost much more in true content than you have gained by
dignity, and that a private gentleman is better attended by a

181 *father* Sir Edward Osborne (1596–1647), commander of the Royalist
forces raised at York during the Civil War.

195 *Earl of Lindsey* Robert Bertie (1582–1642), first earl of Lindsey, Lord
High Admiral of England, was killed at Edgehill while fighting for the
Royalists. His grand-daughter Bridget (1629–1704) married Danby in
1653. She was frequently accused of encouraging his financial mal-
practices.

single servant than your Lordship with so clamorous a train.     210
Pardon me, my Lord, if I speak like a philosopher on this
subject: the fortune which makes a man uneasy cannot make
him happy, and a wise man must think himself uneasy when
few of his actions are in his choice.

This last consideration has brought me to another, and a     215
very seasonable one for your relief, which is, that while I pity
your want of leisure, I have impertinently detained you so
long a time. I have put off my own business, which was my
dedication, till 'tis so late that I am now ashamed to begin it;
and therefore I will say nothing of the poem which I present     220
to you, because I know not if you are like to have an hour
which, with a good conscience, you may throw away in
perusing it. And for the author, I have only to beg the
continuance of your protection to him, who is,

My Lord,

Your Lordship's most obliged

most humble, and most

obedient servant,

JOHN DRYDEN.

# PREFACE

The death of Antony and Cleopatra is a subject which has been
treated by the greatest wits of our nation after Shakespeare, and
by all so variously that their example has given me the confi-
dence to try myself in this bow of Ulysses amongst the crowd
of suitors; and, withal, to take my own measures in aiming at 5
the mark. I doubt not but the same motive has prevailed with
all of us in this attempt: I mean the excellency of the moral, for
the chief persons represented were famous patterns of unlawful
love, and their end accordingly was unfortunate. All reasonable
men have long since concluded that the hero of the poem ought 10
not to be a character of perfect virtue, for then he could not,
without injustice, be made unhappy; nor yet altogether wicked,
because he could not then be pitied: I have therefore steered
the middle course, and have drawn the character of Antony as
favourably as Plutarch, Appian, and Dion Cassius would give 15
me leave; the like I have observed in Cleopatra. That which is
wanting to work up the pity to a greater height was not afforded
me by the story: for the crimes of love which they both com-
mitted were not occasioned by any necessity or fatal ignorance,
but were wholly voluntary, since our passions are, or ought to 20
be, within our power. The fabric of the play is regular enough,
as to the inferior parts of it, and the unities of time, place, and
action more exactly observed than, perhaps, the English theatre
requires. Particularly, the action is so much one that it is the
only of the kind without episode or underplot, every scene in 25
the tragedy conducing to the main design, and every act con-
cluding with a turn of it. The greatest error in the contrivance
seems to be in the person of Octavia; for, though I might use
the privilege of a poet to introduce her into Alexandria, yet I
had not enough considered that the compassion she moved to 30
herself and children was destructive to that which I reserved
for Antony and Cleopatra, whose mutual love, being founded

5 *suitors* Q1, Q2, Q3, W1 (shooters W2)

---

4 *bow of Ulysses* Penelope, Ulysses' wife, after thwarting suitors who assumed that Ulysses was dead, was forced to agree to marry whichever of
them could draw his bow. Ulysses arrived after his prolonged voyage
on the way home from the Trojan war in time to show that he alone
could use the bow, with which he shot them.

upon vice, must lessen the favour of the audience to them, when virtue and innocence were oppressed by it. And, though I justified Antony in some measure by making Octavia's de- 35 parture to proceed wholly from herself, yet the force of the first machine still remained; and the dividing of pity, like the cutting of a river into many channels, abated the strength of the natural stream. But this is an objection which none of my critics have urged against me, and therefore I might have let it 40 pass, if I could have resolved to have been partial to myself. The faults my enemies have found are rather cavils concerning little, and not essential, decencies, which a master of the cere- monies may decide betwixt us. The French poets, I confess, are strict observers of these punctilios. They would not, for 45 example, have suffered Cleopatra and Octavia to have met; or, if they had met, there must only have passed betwixt them some cold civilities, but no eagerness of repartee, for fear of offending against the greatness of their characters, and the modesty of their sex. This objection I foresaw, and at the same 50 time contemned; for I judged it both natural and probable that Octavia, proud of her new-gained conquest, would search out Cleopatra to triumph over her, and that Cleopatra, thus attacked, was not of a spirit to shun the encounter; and 'tis not unlikely that two exasperated rivals should use such satire 55 as I have put into their mouths, for, after all, though the one were a Roman and the other a queen, they were both women. 'Tis true, some actions, though natural, are not fit to be repre- sented, and broad obscenities in words ought in good manners to be avoided: expressions therefore are a modest clothing of 60 our thoughts, as breeches and petticoats are of our bodies. If I have kept myself within the bounds of modesty, all beyond it is but nicety and affectation, which is no more but modesty depraved into a vice. They betray themselves who are too quick of apprehension in such cases, and leave all reasonable men to 65 imagine worse of them than of the poet.

Honest Montaigne goes yet farther: *Nous ne sommes que*

67–76 *Nous ... croît* Montaigne, *Essays*, Book II, chapter xvii (Charles Cotton's translation, 1685): 'We are nothing but ceremony: ceremony carries us away, and we leave the substance of things: we hold by the branches and quit the trunk [and the body]: we have taught the ladies to blush when they hear but that named which they are not at all afraid to do: we dare not call our members by their right names, and are not at all afraid to employ them in all sorts of debauches: ceremony forbids us to express by words things that are lawful and natural, and we obey it; reason forbids us to do things unlawful and ill, and nobody obeys it'. The passage continues: '... for in the study, the subject of which is

*cérémonie; la cérémonie nous emporte, et laissons la substance des choses. Nous nous tenons aux branches, et abandonnons le tronc et le corps. Nous avons appris aux dames de rougir, oyans seulement* 70
*nommer ce qu'elles ne craignent aucunement à faire: nous n'osons appeller à droit nos membres, et ne craignons pas de les employer à toute sorte de débauche. La cérémonie nous défend d'exprimer par paroles les choses licites et naturelles, et nous l'en croyons; la raison nous défend de n'en faire point d'illicites et mauvaises, et* 75
*personne ne l'en croît.* My comfort is that by this opinion, my enemies are but sucking critics, who would fain be nibbling ere their teeth are come.

Yet in this nicety of manners does the excellency of French poetry consist: their heroes are the most civil people breathing, 80
but their good breeding seldom extends to a word of sense; all their wit is in their ceremony; they want the genius which animates our stage; and therefore 'tis but necessary, when they cannot please, that they should take care not to offend. But as the civilest man in the company is commonly the dullest, so these 85
authors, while they are afraid to make you laugh or cry, out of pure good manners make you sleep. They are so careful not to exasperate a critic that they never leave him any work; so busy with the broom, and make so clean a riddance, that there is little left either for censure or for praise: for no part of a poem 90
is worth our discommending where the whole is insipid; as when we have once tasted of palled wine, we stay not to examine it glass by glass. But while they affect to shine in trifles, they are often careless in essentials. Thus their Hippolytus is so scrupulous in point of decency that he will rather 95
expose himself to death than accuse his stepmother to his father, and my critics, I am sure, will commend him for it; but we of grosser apprehensions are apt to think that this excess of generosity is not practicable but with fools and madmen. This was good manners with a vengeance, and the audience is like to 100
be much concerned at the misfortunes of this admirable hero:

---

man, finding so great a variety of judgements, so great a labyrinth of difficulties one upon another, so great diversity and uncertainty, even in the school of wisdom itself: you may judge, seeing those people could not resolve upon the knowledge of themselves and their own condition, which is continually before their eyes and within them, seeing they do not know how that moves which they themselves move, nor how to give us a description of the springs they themselves govern and make use of, how can I believe them about the ebbing and flowing of the Nile?'

94–95 *Hippolytus* a character in Racine's most recent play, *Phèdre*, first performed on 1 January 1677, and published later in the same year.

but take Hippolytus out of his poetic fit, and I suppose he
would think it a wiser part to set the saddle on the right horse,
and choose rather to live with the reputation of a plain-spoken,
honest man, than to die with the infamy of an incestuous villain.    105
In the meantime we may take notice that where the poet ought
to have preserved the character as it was delivered to us by
antiquity, when he should have given us the picture of a rough
young man of the Amazonian strain, a jolly huntsman, and
both by his profession and his early rising a mortal enemy to    110
love, he has chosen to give him the turn of gallantry, sent him
to travel from Athens to Paris, taught him to make love, and
transformed the Hippolytus of Euripides into Monsieur
Hippolyte. I should not have troubled myself thus far with
French poets, but that I find our *Chedreux* critics wholly form    115
their judgements by them. But for my part, I desire to be tried
by the laws of my own country; for it seems unjust to me that
the French should prescribe here till they have conquered.
Our little sonneteers who follow them have too narrow souls
to judge of poetry. Poets themselves are the most proper,    120
though I conclude not the only, critics. But till some genius as
universal as Aristotle shall arise, one who can penetrate into all
arts and sciences without the practice of them, I shall think
it reasonable that the judgement of an artificer in his own art
should be preferable to the opinion of another man, at least    125
where he is not bribed by interest or prejudiced by malice.
And this, I suppose, is manifest by plain induction. For, first,
the crowd cannot be presumed to have more than a gross
instinct of what pleases or displeases them: every man will
grant me this; but then, by a particular kindness to himself, he    130
draws his own stake first, and will be distinguished from the
multitude, of which other men may think him one. But if I
come closer to those who are allowed for witty men, either by
the advantage of their quality or by common fame, and affirm
that neither are they qualified to decide sovereignly concerning    135
poetry, I shall yet have a strong party of my opinion; for most
of them severally will exclude the rest, either from the number
of witty men, or at least of able judges; but here again they are
all indulgent to themselves, and everyone who believes himself
a wit, that is, every man, will pretend at the same time to a    140
right of judging. But to press it yet farther, there are many

122 *one* Q1, W2 (om. Q2, Q3, W1)

---

115 *Chedreux* a wig of a particular style, named after its French maker.

witty men, but few poets; neither have all poets a taste of tragedy. And this is the rock on which they are daily splitting.
Poetry, which is a picture of nature, must generally please; but
'tis not to be understood that all parts of it must please every      145
man; therefore is not tragedy to be judged by a witty man
whose taste is only confined to comedy. Nor is every man who
loves tragedy a sufficient judge of it; he must understand the
excellencies of it too, or he will only prove a blind admirer, not
a critic. From hence it comes that so many satires on poets, and    150
censures of their writings, fly abroad. Men of pleasant conver-
sation (at least esteemed so), and indued with a trifling kind of
fancy, perhaps helped out with some smattering of Latin, are
ambitious to distinguish themselves from the herd of gentlemen
by their poetry:                                                      155

> Rarus enim ferme sensus communis in illa
> Fortuna.

And is not this a wretched affectation, not to be contented with
what Fortune has done for them, and sit down quietly with
their estates, but they must call their wits in question, and      160
needlessly expose their nakedness to public view, not considering that they are not to expect the same approbation from
sober men which they have found from their flatterers after the
third bottle? If a little glittering in discourse has passed them
on us for witty men, where was the necessity of undeceiving       165
the world? Would a man who has an ill title to an estate, but
yet is in possession of it, would he bring it of his own accord to
be tried at Westminster? We who write, if we want the talent,
yet have the excuse that we do it for a poor subsistence; but
what can be urged in their defence who, not having the           170
vocation of poverty to scribble, out of mere wantonness take
pains to make themselves ridiculous? Horace was certainly in

144 *picture of nature* In *Of Dramatic Poesy* a play is defined as 'a just and
    lively image of human nature, representing its passions and humours,
    and the changes of fortune to which it is subject; for the delight and
    instruction of mankind' (Kinsley and Parfitt, op. cit., p. 25).
156–7 *Rarus . . . Fortuna.* Juvenal, *Satires*, VIII, 73–4: '. . . We seldom
    find/Much sense with an exalted fortune joined' (Stepney's translation
    in Dryden's *Juvenal*, 1693).
161 *nakedness* Sir Charles Sedley and others appeared naked on the balcony
    of a tavern in London on 16 June 1663. In 1677, John Wilmot, 2nd earl
    of Rochester, and his guests were reported to have run naked through
    Woodstock Park.
168 *Westminster* Westminster Hall, part of Westminster Palace, was the
    principal seat of justice from the thirteenth to the nineteenth century.
172 Horace, *Satires*, I, i, 1–3.

the right where he said that 'no man is satisfied with his own
condition'. A poet is not pleased because he is not rich; and the
rich are discontented because the poets will not admit them of    175
their number. Thus the case is hard with writers: if they
succeed not, they must starve; and if they do, some malicious
satire is prepared to level them for daring to please without
their leave. But while they are so eager to destroy the fame of
others, their ambition is manifest in their concernment: some     180
poem of their own is to be produced, and the slaves are to be
laid flat with their faces on the ground, that the monarch may
appear in the greater majesty.

Dionysius and Nero had the same longings, but with all their
power they could never bring their business well about. 'Tis      185
true, they proclaimed themselves poets by sound of trumpet;
and poets they were, upon pain of death to any man who durst
call them otherwise. The audience had a fine time on't, you
may imagine: they sat in a bodily fear, and looked as demurely as
they could, for 'twas a hanging matter to laugh unseasonably,     190
and the tyrants were suspicious, as they had reason, that their
subjects had 'em in the wind: so every man, in his own defence,
set as good a face upon the business as he could: 'twas known
beforehand that the monarchs were to be crowned laureates;
but when the show was over, and an honest man was suffered        195
to depart quietly, he took out his laughter which he had
stifled, with a firm resolution never more to see an emperor's
play, though he had been ten years a-making it. In the meantime, the true poets were they who made the best markets,
for they had wit enough to yield the prize with a good grace,     200
and not contend with him who had thirty legions: they were
sure to be rewarded if they confessed themselves bad writers,
and that was somewhat better than to be martyrs for their
reputation. Lucan's example was enough to teach them manners; and after he was put to death for overcoming Nero, the      205

---

184 *Dionysius and Nero* Dionysius I (*c.* 430–367 B.C.), tyrant of Syracuse,
and Nero Claudius Caesar (A.D. 37–68), emperor of Rome from
A.D. 54 to 68, both fancied themselves poets despite an apparent lack of
talent, and won acclaim through the use of their power.
201 *thirty legions* Montaigne, *Essays*, III, chapter vii includes this passage
(Cotton's translation): 'the Emperor Adrian disputing with the
philosopher Favorinus about the interpretation of some word,
Favorinus soon yielded him the victory; for which his friends rebuking
him; 'You talk simply', said he; 'would you not have him wiser than I
who commands thirty legions?'.
204 *Lucan* Montaigne (*Essays*, II, chapter viii) says that Lucan was per-
secuted for his learning. In fact, Lucan (A.D. 39–65), after winning a

emperor carried it without dispute for the best poet in his dominions. No man was ambitious of that grinning honour, for if he heard the malicious trumpeter proclaiming his name before his betters, he knew there was but one way with him. Maecenas took another course, and we know he was more than 210 a great man, for he was witty too; but finding himself far gone in poetry, which Seneca assures us was not his talent, he thought it his best way to be well with Virgil and with Horace, that at least he might be a poet at the second hand; and we see how happily it has succeeded with him, for his own bad poetry 215 is forgotten, and their panegyrics of him still remain. But they who should be our patrons are for no such expensive ways to fame: they have much of the poetry of Maecenas, but little of his liberality. They are for persecuting Horace and Virgil in the persons of their successors (for such is every man who has 220 any part of their soul and fire, though in a less degree). Some of their little zanies yet go farther, for they are persecutors even of Horace himself, as far as they are able, by their ignorant and vile imitations of him, by making an unjust use of his authority, and turning his artillery against his friends. But how 225 would he disdain to be copied by such hands! I dare answer for

219 *persecuting* ... *Virgil* Q1, Q2, Q3, W2 (procuring themselves reputation W1)

---

prize for a poem in praise of Nero in A.D. 60, was forced to commit suicide because of his complicity in the Piso conspiracy.

207 *grinning honour* In *1 Henry IV* Falstaff says of the dead Sir Walter Blunt: 'I like not such grinning honour as Sir Walter hath' (V. iii, 58).

210 *Maecenas* Seneca, *Epistulae Morales*, 114, 4–8. Seneca describes Maecenas (see *All For Love*, III, 68) as a man whose loose living marred his greatness.

213 *Horace* According to David M. Vieth (*The Complete Poems of John Wilmot, Earl of Rochester*, New Haven and London, 1968, p. 120), Rochester's *An Allusion to Horace, the Tenth Satire of the First Book* was written during the winter of 1675–76 and circulated in manuscript. Dryden is one of the main objects of his satire, and is attacked among other things for his attitude to Shakespeare and his contemporaries:
> But does not Dryden find ev'n Jonson dull;
> Fletcher and Beaumont uncorrect, and full
> Of lewd lines, as he calls 'em; Shakespeare's style
> Stiff and affected; to his own the while
> Allowing all the justness that his pride
> So arrogantly had to these denied? (ll. 81–6).

222 *zanies* Zanni, the *Commedia dell'Arte* servant who imitates his master's actions with ridiculous incompetence.

him, he would be more uneasy in their company than he was with Crispinus, their forefather, in the Holy Way, and would no more have allowed them a place amongst the critics than he would Demetrius the mimic and Tigellius the buffoon: 230

> *Demetri, teque, Tigelli,*
> *Discipulorum inter jubeo plorare cathedras.*

With what scorn would he look down on such miserable translators, who make doggerel of his Latin, mistake his meaning, misapply his censures, and often contradict their own! He 235 is fixed as a landmark to set out the bounds of poetry,

> *Saxum antiquum ingens, ...*
> *Limes agro positus, litem ut discerneret arvis.*

But other arms than theirs, and other sinews, are required to raise the weight of such an author; and when they would 240 toss him against their enemies,

> *Genua labant, gelidus concrevit frigore sanguis,*
> *Tum lapis ipse viri vacuum per inane volutus,*
> *Nec spatium evasit totum neque pertulit ictum.*

228 *Crispinus* In *Satires*, I, iv, 14–16, Crispinus challenges Horace to a competition to see who can write more quickly, and in *Satires* I, ix, Horace meets in the Via Sacra with a self-important would-be poet who boasts that he can write faster than anyone else. The fairly obvious identification of this poet with Crispinus is made in Jonson's *The Poetaster*.

231 *Demetri ... Tigelli* Demetrius is identified by Porphyrio with the ape who repeats Calvus and Catullus in *Satires*, I, x, 18, and also trained actresses (Rochester was reputedly responsible for bringing Elizabeth Barry to the stage). Hermogenes Tigellius is described by Horace as a singer (*Satires*, I, ii and iii) and a fop (I, x, 17). The passage quoted (which normally reads 'discipularum') is *Satires*, I, x, 90–1. Rochester does not include any version of these lines in the *Imitation*: 'Demetrius, and you, Tigellius, I bid you go and whine among your pupils' easy chairs'. The theme of this satire is partly the inadequacy of some people's judgement of poetry.

237–8 *Saxum ... arvis Aeneid*, XII, 897–8, the description of the battle between Aeneas and Turnus, king of the Rutulians.

> An antique stone he saw: the common bound
> Of neighb'ring fields, and barrier of the ground ...
> (Dryden's translation ll. 1300–1; *Poems*, III, 1421).

242–4 *Genua ... ictum Aeneid*, XII, 905–7, the continuation of the above passage. Turnus attempts to throw the rock at Aeneas:

> His knocking knees are bent beneath the load,
> And shivering cold congeals his vital blood.
> The stone drops from his arms, and, falling short
> For want of vigour, mocks his vain effort.
> (ibid., ll. 1308–11).

For my part, I would wish no other revenge, either for my-    245
self or the rest of the poets, from this rhyming judge of the
twelvepenny gallery, this legitimate son of Sternhold, than that
he would subscribe his name to his censure, or (not to tax him
beyond his learning) set his mark. For should he own himself
publicly, and come from behind the lion's skin, they whom he    250
condemns would be thankful to him, they whom he praises
would choose to be condemned, and the magistrates whom he
has elected would modestly withdraw from their employment
to avoid the scandal of his nomination. The sharpness of his
satire, next to himself, falls most heavily on his friends, and    255
they ought never to forgive him for commending them per-
petually the wrong way, and sometimes by contraries. If he
have a friend whose hastiness in writing is his greatest fault,
Horace would have taught him to have minced the matter, and
to have called it readiness of thought and a flowing fancy; for    260
friendship will allow a man to christen an imperfection by the
name of some neighbour virtue:

> *Vellem in amicitia sic erraremus, et isti*
> *Errori nomen virtus posuisset honestum.*

247 *twelvepenny gallery* the cheapest seats in the theatre.
247 *Sternhold* Thomas Sternhold (d. 1594) and John Hopkins (d. 1570) produced verse paraphrases of the Psalms. They were taken as types of the
   bad poet: see, for instance, *The Second Part of Absalom and Achitophel*,
   l. 403.
250 *lion's skin* Aesop's fable of the ass who dressed himself in a lion's skin but
   betrayed his identity by braying. See also the quotation from Juvenal,
   l. 269 below.
252 *magistrates* Rochester's *Allusion to Horace* ends:
   I loathe the rabble; 'tis enough for me
   If Sedley, Shadwell, Shepherd, Wycherley,
   Godolphin, Butler, Buckhurst, Buckingham,
   And some few more, whom I omit to name,
   Approve my sense: I count their censure fame.
                              (ll. 120–5, *Complete Poems*, p. 126).
263–4 *Vellem . . . honestum* Horace, *Satires*, I, iii, 41–2. After pointing out
   how a lover may not only be blind to his love's failings, but may even be
   attracted by them, he says: 'I could wish that we made the same mistake
   in friendship, and that our moral code gave an honourable name to such
   an error'.

But he would never have allowed him to have called a slow man 265
hasty, or a hasty writer a slow drudge, as Juvenal explains it:

> *Canibus pigris scabieque vetusta*
> *Levibus et siccae lambentibus ora lucernae*
> *Nomen erit pardus, tigris, leo, si quid adhuc est*
> *Quod fremit in terris violentius.* 270

Yet Lucretius laughs at a foolish lover even for excusing the
imperfections of his mistress:

> *Nigra melichrus est, immunda et foetida acosmos.*
> *Balba loqui non quit, traulizi; muta pudens est, etc.*

But to drive it *ad Aethiopem cygnum* is not to be endured. I 275
leave him to interpret this by the benefit of his French version
on the other side, and without farther considering him than I
have the rest of my illiterate censors, whom I have disdained to
answer because they are not qualified for judges. It remains
that I acquaint the reader that I have endeavoured in this play 280
to follow the practice of the ancients, who, as Mr Rymer has

265–6 *slow man . . . drudge* Rochester, *An Allusion to Horace*, ll. 41–3:
        Of all our modern wits, none seems to me
        Once to have touched upon true comedy
        But hasty Shadwell and slow Wycherley.
                        (*Complete Poems*, pp. 122–3)
267–70 *Canibus . . . violentius* Juvenal, *Satires*, VIII, 34–7: 'Lazy curs, bald
        with chronic mange, who lick the edges of a dry lamp, will hear the
        names of "Leopard", "Tiger", "Lion", or of whatever else in the world
        roars more fiercely'. The passage concludes: 'Be therefore careful, lest
        the world in jest/Should thee just so with a mock-title greet'. (Stepney's
        translation). There follows an attack on Rubellius Blandus for his pride
        solely in his kinship to Nero, from which the quotation (ll. 156–7, above
        is taken.
273–4 *Nigra . . . est, etc.* Lucretius, *De Rerum Natura*, IV, 1160, 1164.
        The sallow skin is for the swarthy put,
        And love can make a slattern of a slut . . .
        She stammers, oh what grace in lisping lies;
        If she says nothing, to be sure she's wise.
                        (Dryden's translation, ll. 145–6, 151–2; *Poems*, I, 417).
275 *ad Aethiopem cygnum* Juvenal, *Satires*, VIII, 33 (the start of the passage
        quoted above (l. 267): '[to call] an Ethiope a swan'). When Rochester,
        banished from the Court, returned to London disguised as a mounte-
        bank, he set up shop next to an inn called the Black Swan.
281 *Rymer The Tragedies of the Last Age Considered and Examined by the
        Practice of the Ancients and by the Common Sense of All Ages* by Thomas
        Rymer (1641–1713) was published just before *All For Love* in 1678.

judiciously observed, are, and ought to be, our masters. Horace likewise gives it for a rule in his art of poetry,

> *Vos exemplaria Graeca*
> *Nocturna versate manu, versate diurna.* 285

Yet, though their models are regular, they are too little for English tragedy, which requires to be built in a larger compass. I could give an instance in the *Oedipus Tyrannus*, which was the masterpiece of Sophocles, but I reserve it for a more fit occasion, which I hope to have hereafter. In my style I have 290 professed to imitate the divine Shakespeare, which that I might perform more freely, I have disencumbered myself from rhyme. Not that I condemn my former way, but that this is more proper to my present purpose. I hope I need not to explain myself, that I have not copied my author servilely: words and 295 phrases must of necessity receive a change in succeeding ages, but 'tis almost a miracle that much of his language remains so pure, and that he who began dramatic poetry amongst us, un- taught by any and, as Ben Jonson tells us, without learning, should by the force of his own genius perform so much that in 300 a manner he has left no praise for any who come after him. The occasion is fair, and the subject would be pleasant, to handle the difference of styles betwixt him and Fletcher, and wherein and how far they are both to be imitated. But since I must not be over-confident of my own performance after him, it will be 305 prudence in me to be silent. Yet I hope I may affirm, and with- out vanity, that by imitating him I have excelled myself through- out the play; and particularly, that I prefer the scene betwixt Antony and Ventidius in the first act to anything which I have written in this kind. 310

---

284–5 *Vos . . . diurna* Horace, *Ars Poetica*, ll. 268–9. 'For yourselves, study greek models by day, study them by night'.

288 *Oedipus Tyrannus* Dryden collaborated with Nathaniel Lee in writing *Oedipus*, based on the plays of Sophocles, Seneca, and Corneille, staged in September 1678, and published in 1679.

299 *Jonson* In *To the Memory of my Beloved, The Author Mr. William Shakespeare* in the First Folio, Jonson wrote: 'And though thou hadst small Latin and less Greek . . .' (l. 31).

303 *Fletcher* In terms purely of frequency of production during the Restora- tion period, the plays of Beaumont and Fletcher were more popular than the plays of any other Elizabethan or Jacobean dramatist. A comparison of Shakespeare and Fletcher is made by Dryden in 'The Grounds of Criticism in Tragedy', part of the Preface to *Troilus and Cressida* (1679).

# PROLOGUE TO ANTONY AND CLEOPATRA

What flocks of critics hover here today,  
As vultures wait on armies for their prey,  
All gaping for the carcass of a play!  
With croaking notes they bode some dire event,  
And follow dying poets by the scent.                                    5  
Ours gives himself for gone: y'have watched your time!  
He fights this day unarmed, without his rhyme,  
And brings a tale which often has been told,  
As sad as Dido's, and almost as old.  
His hero, whom you wits his bully call,                                 10  
Bates of his mettle, and scarce rants at all.  
He's somewhat lewd, but a well-meaning mind;  
Weeps much, fights little, but is wondrous kind;  
In short, a pattern and companion fit  
For all the keeping tonies of the pit.                                 15  
I could name more: a wife, and mistress too,  
Both (to be plain) too good for most of you;  
The wife well-natured, and the mistress true.  
Now, poets, if your fame has been his care,  
Allow him all the candour you can spare.                               20  
A brave man scorns to quarrel once a day,  
Like hectors in at every petty fray.  
Let those find fault whose wit's so very small,  
They've need to show that they can think at all:  
Errors, like straws, upon the surface flow;                            25  
He who would search for pearls must dive below.  
Fops may have leave to level all they can,  
As pygmies would be glad to lop a man.  
Half-wits are fleas, so little and so light  
We scarce could know they live but that they bite.                     30  
But as the rich, when tired with daily feasts,  
For change become their next poor tenant's guests,  
Drink hearty draughts of ale from plain brown bowls,  
And snatch the homely rasher from the coals;  
So you, retiring from much better cheer,                               35  

---

15 *tonies* fools, simpletons (a 17th-century coinage) with a pun on
Antony's name.
22 *hectors* bullies.

For once may venture to do penance here.
And since that plenteous autumn now is past
Whose grapes and peaches have indulged your taste,
Take in good part, from our poor poet's board,
Such rivelled fruits as winter can afford.      40

40 *rivelled* wrinkled

## PERSONS REPRESENTED

|  | By |
|---|---|
| MARC ANTONY, | *Mr Hart* |
| VENTIDIUS, *his general*, | *Mr Mohun* |
| DOLLABELLA, *his friend*, | *Mr Clarke* |
| ALEXAS, *the Queen's eunuch*, | *Mr Goodman* |
| SERAPION, *Priest of Isis*, | *Mr Griffin* |
| [MYRIS,] *another priest* | *Mr Coysh* |
| SERVANTS OF ANTONY, [PRIESTS] | |
| CLEOPATRA, *Queen of Egypt*, | *Mrs Boutell* |
| OCTAVIA, *Antony's wife*, | *Mrs Corey* |
| CHARMION ⎫ *Cleopatra's Maids* | |
| IRAS ⎭ | |
| ANTONY'S TWO LITTLE DAUGHTERS | |

# ALL FOR LOVE,

## or

## The World Well Lost

### Act I

*Scene, The Temple of Isis*
*Enter* SERAPION, MYRIS, *Priests of Isis*

SERAPION

    Portents and prodigies are grown so frequent
    That they have lost their name. Our fruitful Nile
    Flowed ere the wonted season, with a torrent
    So unexpected and so wondrous fierce
    That the wild deluge overtook the haste          5
    Even of the hinds that watched it: men and beasts
    Were borne above the tops of trees that grew
    On th'utmost margin of the watermark.
    Then with so swift an ebb the flood drove backward,
    It slipped from underneath the scaly herd:       10
    Here monstrous *phocae* panted on the shore;
    Forsaken dolphins there with their broad tails
    Lay lashing the departing waves; hard by 'em,
    Sea-horses floundering in the slimy mud
    Tossed up their heads and dashed the ooze about 'em.   15

*Enter* ALEXAS *behind them*

MYRIS

    Avert these omens, Heaven!
SERAPION

    Last night, between the hours of twelve and one,
    In a lone aisle o'th'temple while I walked,
    A whirlwind rose, that with a violent blast

s.d. *Isis* the Egyptian goddess of fertility, the wife of Osiris, god of death
(see V, 66).
11 *phocae* seals.
14 *Sea-horses* hippopotami.

23

Shook all the dome: the doors around me clapped;                    20
The iron wicket that defends the vault
Where the long race of Ptolemies is laid
Burst open, and disclosed the mighty dead.
From out each monument, in order placed,
An armèd ghost start up; the boy-king last                    25
Reared his inglorious head. A peal of groans
Then followed, and a lamentable voice
Cried, 'Egypt is no more!' My blood ran back,
My shaking knees against each other knocked;
On the cold pavement down I fell entranced,                    30
And so unfinished left the horrid scene.

ALEXAS *showing himself*
And dreamed you this, or did invent the story
To frighten our Egyptian boys withal,
And train 'em up betimes in fear of priesthood?

SERAPION
My Lord, I saw you not,                    35
Nor meant my words should reach your ears; but what
I uttered was most true.

ALEXAS                    A foolish dream,
Bred from the fumes of indigested feasts
And holy luxury.

SERAPION            I know my duty:
This goes no farther.

ALEXAS                    'Tis not fit it should;                    40
Nor would the times now bear it, were it true.
All southern, from yon hills, the Roman camp
Hangs o'er us black and threatening, like a storm
Just breaking on our heads.

SERAPION
Our faint Egyptians pray for Antony,                    45
But in their servile hearts they own Octavius.

MYRIS
Why then does Antony dream out his hours,
And tempts not Fortune for a noble day
Which might redeem what Actium lost?

ALEXAS
He thinks 'tis past recovery.

---

25 *start* Q1, Q2, Q3 (starts W1, W2)
34 *'em* Q1, Q2, Q3, W2 (om. W1)

---

25 *boy-king* Ptolemy XIV, the last of the Ptolemies to rule Egypt, was killed
at the age of 15 in 44 B.C. on Cleopatra's orders.

SERAPION                    Yet the foe                        50
  Seems not to press the siege.
ALEXAS                          Oh, there's the wonder.
  Maecenas and Agrippa, who can most
  With Caesar, are his foes. His wife Octavia,
  Driven from his house, solicits her revenge;
  And Dollabella, who was once his friend,              55
  Upon some private grudge now seeks his ruin:
  Yet still war seems on either side to sleep.
SERAPION
  'Tis strange that Antony for some days past
  Has not beheld the face of Cleopatra,
  But here in Isis' temple lives retired,              60
  And makes his heart a prey to black despair.
ALEXAS
  'Tis true; and we much fear he hopes by absence
  To cure his mind of love.
SERAPION                      If he be vanquished
  Or make his peace, Egypt is doomed to be
  A Roman province, and our plenteous harvests          65
  Must then redeem the scarceness of their soil.
  While Antony stood firm, our Alexandria
  Rivalled proud Rome (dominion's other seat),
  And Fortune, striding like a vast Colossus,
  Could fix an equal foot of empire here.               70
ALEXAS
  Had I my wish, these tyrants of all nature
  Who lord it o'er mankind, should perish, perish,
  Each by the other's sword; but since our will
  Is lamely followed by our power, we must
  Depend on one, with him to rise or fall.              75
SERAPION
  How stands the Queen affected?
ALEXAS                              Oh, she dotes,
  She dotes, Serapion, on this vanquished man,
  And winds herself about his mighty ruins,
  Whom would she yet forsake, yet yield him up,
  This hunted prey, to his pursuer's hands,            80
  She might preserve us all; but 'tis in vain—
  This changes my designs, this blasts my counsels,

---

72 *perish, perish* Q1 corrected, Q2, Q3, W1, W2 (perish, here Q1 uncorrected)

69 *Colossus* The Colossus of Rhodes straddled the entrance to the harbour;
  cf. *Julius Caesar*, I. ii, 135–6: 'Why, man, he doth bestride the narrow
  world/Like a Colossus . . .'

And makes me use all means to keep him here,
Whom I could wish divided from her arms
Far as the earth's deep centre. Well you know          85
The state of things; no more of your ill omens
And black prognostics: labour to confirm
The people's hearts.

*Enter* VENTIDIUS, *talking aside with a*
          GENTLEMAN *of Antony's*

SERAPION                    These Romans will o'erhear us.
But who's that stranger? By his warlike port,
His fierce demeanour and erected look,                  90
He's of no vulgar note.
ALEXAS                    Oh, 'tis Ventidius,
Our Emperor's great lieutenant in the East,
Who first showed Rome that Parthia could be conquered.
When Antony returned from Syria last,
He left this man to guard the Roman frontiers.          95
SERAPION
You seem to know him well.
ALEXAS
Too well. I saw him in Cilicia first,
When Cleopatra there met Antony:
A mortal foe he was to us, and Egypt.
But, let me witness to the worth I hate,                100
A braver Roman never drew a sword;
Firm to his prince, but as a friend, not slave.
He ne'er was of his pleasures, but presides
O'er all his cooler hours and morning counsels.
In short, the plainness, fierceness, rugged virtue      105
Of an old true-stamped Roman lives in him.
His coming bodes I know not what of ill
To our affairs. Withdraw to mark him better,
And I'll acquaint you why I sought you here,
And what's our present work.

*They withdraw to a corner of the stage; and* VENTIDIUS, *with
          the other, comes forwards to the front*

VENTIDIUS                    Not see him, say you?       110
I say I must, and will.
GENTLEMAN              He has commanded,
On pain of death, none should approach his presence.

VENTIDIUS
  I bring him news will raise his drooping spirits,
  Give him new life.
GENTLEMAN          He sees not Cleopatra.
VENTIDIUS
  Would he had never seen her.                                    115
GENTLEMAN
  He eats not, drinks not, sleeps not, has no use
  Of anything but thought; or, if he talks,
  'Tis to himself, and then 'tis perfect raving:
  Then he defies the world, and bids it pass;
  Sometimes he gnaws his lip, and curses loud                     120
  The boy Octavius; then he draws his mouth
  Into a scornful smile, and cries, 'Take all,
  The world's not worth my care'.
VENTIDIUS               Just, just his nature.
  Virtue's his path; but sometimes 'tis too narrow
  For his vast soul, and then he starts out wide                   125
  And bounds into a vice that bears him far
  From his first course, and plunges him in ills:
  But when his danger makes him find his fault,
  Quick to observe and full of sharp remorse,
  He censures eagerly his own misdeeds,                            130
  Judging himself with malice to himself,
  And not forgiving what as man he did
  Because his other parts are more than man.
  He must not thus be lost.

ALEXAS *and the* PRIESTS *come forward*

ALEXAS
  You have your full instructions, now advance:                  135
  Proclaim your orders loudly.
SERAPION
  Romans, Egyptians, hear the Queen's command!
  Thus Cleopatra bids: 'Let labour cease;
  To pomp and triumphs give this happy day

---

113 *drooping spirits* cf. *1 Henry VI*, V. ii, 1: 'These news, my lords, may
    cheer our drooping spirits'. S. Klima, 'Some unrecorded borrowings
    from Shakespeare in Dryden's *All For Love*', *N & Q*, 208 (1963),
    415–18.
121 *boy Octavius* Octavius Caesar (63 B.C.–A.D. 14) was twenty years
    younger than Antony (*c.* 83–30 B.C.).
129 *sharp remorse* See Introduction, p. xv.

That gave the world a lord: 'tis Antony's'.                    140
Live Antony; and Cleopatra live!
Be this the general voice sent up to heaven,
And every public place repeat this echo.

VENTIDIUS *aside*
Fine pageantry.

SERAPION              Set out before your doors
The images of all your sleeping fathers,                    145
With laurels crowned; with laurels wreathe your posts,
And strow with flowers the pavement; let the priests
Do present sacrifice; pour out the wine,
And call the gods to join with you in gladness.

VENTIDIUS
Curse on the tongue that bids this general joy!                    150
Can they be friends of Antony, who revel
When Antony's in danger? Hide, for shame,
You Romans, your great grandsires' images,
For fear their souls should animate their marbles
To blush at their degenerate progeny.                    155

ALEXAS
A love which knows no bounds to Antony
Would mark the day with honours when all Heaven
Laboured for him, when each propitious star
Stood wakeful in his orb to watch that hour,
And shed his better influence. Her own birthday                    160
Our Queen neglected, like a vulgar fate
That passed obscurely by.

VENTIDIUS                    Would it had slept
Divided far from his, till some remote
And future age had called it out to ruin
Some other prince, not him.

ALEXAS                    Your emperor,                    165
Though grown unkind, would be more gentle than
T"upbraid my Queen for loving him too well.

VENTIDIUS
Does the mute sacrifice upbraid the priest?
He knows him not his executioner.
Oh, she has decked his ruin with her love,                    170
Led him in golden bands to gaudy slaughter,
And made perdition pleasing: she has left him

---

145 *images . . . fathers* the *Lares Familiares*, spirits, sometimes thought to be
those of ancestors, who had special care over the home, and who were
worshipped on all occasions of importance.

The blank of what he was.
I tell thee, eunuch, she has quite unmanned him.
Can any Roman see and know him now,                    175
Thus altered from the lord of half mankind,
Unbent, unsinewed, made a woman's toy,
Shrunk from the vast extent of all his honours,
And cramped within a corner of the world?
O Antony!                    180
Thou bravest soldier, and thou best of friends!
Bounteous as Nature; next to Nature's God!
Couldst thou but make new worlds, so wouldst thou give 'em,
As bounty were thy being. Rough in battle
As the first Romans when they went to war;                    185
Yet, after victory, more pitiful
Than all their praying virgins left at home!

ALEXAS
Would you could add to those more shining virtues
His truth to her who loves him.
VENTIDIUS                                Would I could not.
But wherefore waste I precious hours with thee?                    190
Thou art her darling mischief, her chief engine,
Antony's other fate. Go, tell thy Queen
Ventidius is arrived to end her charms.
Let your Egyptian timbrels play alone,
Nor mix effeminate sounds with Roman trumpets.                    195
You dare not fight for Antony; go pray,
And keep your cowards' holiday in temples.
                    (*Exeunt* ALEXAS, SERAPION)


[*Enter another*] GENTLEMAN *of Marc Antony*


SECOND GENTLEMAN
The Emperor approaches and commands,
On pain of death, that none presume to stay.
FIRST GENTLEMAN
I dare not disobey him.                    (*Going out with the other*)
VENTIDIUS                    Well, I dare.                    200
But I'll observe him first unseen, and find
Which way his humour drives. The rest I'll venture.
                    (*Withdraws*)


174 *quite* Q1, W2 (om. Q2, Q3, W1)
197 s.d. *Enter another* ed. (*Re-enter the* Q1)
202 *The rest* Q1, Q2, W2 (om. Q3, W1)

*Enter* ANTONY, *walking with a disturbed motion before he speaks*

ANTONY
    They tell me 'tis my birthday, and I'll keep it
    With double pomp of sadness.
    'Tis what the day deserves which gave me breath.    205
    Why was I raised the meteor of the world,
    Hung in the skies, and blazing as I travelled,
    Till all my fires were spent, and then cast downward
    To be trod out by Caesar?
VENTIDIUS *aside*               On my soul,
    'Tis mournful, wondrous mournful!
ANTONY               Count thy gains.    210
    Now, Antony, wouldst thou be born for this?
    Glutton of fortune, thy devouring youth
    Has starved thy wanting age.
VENTIDIUS *aside*        How sorrow shakes him!
    So, now the tempest tears him up by th'roots,
    And on the ground extends the noble ruin.    215
ANTONY *having thrown himself down*
    Lie there, thou shadow of an emperor:
    The place thou pressest on thy mother earth
    Is all thy empire now; now it contains thee:
    Some few days hence, and then 'twill be too large,
    When thou'rt contracted in thy narrow urn,    220
    Shrunk to a few cold ashes. Then Octavia
    (For Cleopatra will not live to see it),
    Octavia then will have thee all her own,
    And bear thee in her widowed hand to Caesar;
    Caesar will weep, the crocodile will weep,    225
    To see his rival of the universe
    Lie still and peaceful there. I'll think no more on't.

---

216 s.d. ANTONY . . . *down* Q1, Q2, Q3, W2 (W1 takes this as a stage direction
    only, rather than as a speech prefix, and gives ll. 216–27 to Ventidius and
    228–40 to Antony)

---

216–21 *Lie . . . ashes* cf. *1 Henry IV*, V. iv, 88–92:
    Ill-weaved ambition, how much art thou shrunk!
    When that this body did contain a spirit,
    A kingdom for it was too small a bound;
    But now two paces of the vilest earth
    Is room enough            (Klima).

Give me some music; look that it be sad.
I'll soothe my melancholy till I swell
And burst myself with sighing.        (*Soft music*)   230
'Tis somewhat to my humour. Stay, I fancy
I'm now turned wild, a commoner of Nature;
Of all forsaken, and forsaking all,
Live in a shady forest's sylvan scene,
Stretched at my length beneath some blasted oak;          235
I lean my head upon the mossy bark,
And look just of a piece, as I grew from it;
My uncombed locks, matted like mistletoe,
Hang o'er my hoary face; a murmuring brook
Runs at my foot.
VENTIDIUS          Methinks I fancy                    240
    Myself there too.
ANTONY          The herd come jumping by me,
    And, fearless, quench their thirst while I look on,
    And take me for their fellow-citizen.
    More of this image, more; it lulls my thoughts.
                                     (*Soft music again*)

VENTIDIUS
    I must disturb him; I can hold no longer.           245
                                     (*Stands before him*)

ANTONY *starting up*
    Art thou Ventidius?
VENTIDIUS          Are you Antony?
    I'm liker what I was than you to him
    I left you last.
ANTONY          I'm angry.
VENTIDIUS          So am I.


244 *it* Q1, Q2, W2 (om. Q3, W1)

---

228–30 *Give . . . sighing* cf. *Twelfth Night*, I. i, 1–3:
        If music be the food of love, play on,
        Give me excess of it, that, surfeiting,
        The appetite may sicken and so die.
231–43 *Stay . . . fellow-citizen* '. . . he lived an exile from men, and declared
        that he was contentedly imitating the life of Timon' (Plutarch, p. 297).
        Dryden builds on this suggestion by borrowing not from *Timon of
        Athens* but from *As You Like It*, II. i, 29–63, particularly ll. 30–2
        ('. . . he lay along/Under an oak whose antique root peeps out/Upon
        the brook . . .') and ll. 52–5 ('Anon, a careless herd,/Full of the pasture,
        jumps along by him/And never stays to greet him "Ay", quoth Jaques,/
        "Sweep on, you fat and greasy citizens"';).

ANTONY
  I would be private: leave me.
VENTIDIUS                         Sir, I love you,
  And therefore will not leave you.
ANTONY                         Will not leave me?                         250
  Where have you learnt that answer? Who am I?
VENTIDIUS
  My Emperor; the man I love next Heaven;
  If I said more, I think 'twere scarce a sin:
  Y'are all that's good, and god-like.
ANTONY                         All that's wretched.
  You will not leave me then?
VENTIDIUS                         'Twas too presuming                     255
  To say I would not, but I dare not leave you;
  And 'tis unkind in you to chide me hence
  So soon, when I so far have come to see you.
ANTONY
  Now thou hast seen me, art thou satisfied?
  For, if a friend, thou hast beheld enough;                             260
  And, if a foe, too much.
VENTIDIUS weeping
  Look, Emperor, this is no common dew.
  I have not wept this forty year, but now
  My mother comes afresh into my eyes;
  I cannot help her softness.                                            265
ANTONY
  By Heaven, he weeps, poor good old man, he weeps!
  The big round drops course one another down
  The furrows of his cheeks. Stop 'em, Ventidius,
  Or I shall blush to death: they set my shame,
  That caused 'em, full before me.
VENTIDIUS                         I'll do my best.                        270
ANTONY
  Sure there's contagion in the tears of friends:
  See, I have caught it too. Believe me, 'tis not
  For my own griefs, but thine.—Nay, father.
VENTIDIUS                                         Emperor.
ANTONY
  Emperor! Why, that's the style of victory.
  The conquering soldier, red with unfelt wounds,                        275

254 *god-like* W2 (good-like Q1, Q2, Q3, W1)
259 *me* Q1, Q2, W2 (om. Q3, W1)
260 *thou hast beheld* Q1, Q2, W2 (thou hast seen me, beheld Q3, W1)

Salutes his general so; but never more
Shall that sound reach my ears.
VENTIDIUS                              I warrant you.
ANTONY
Actium, Actium! Oh—
VENTIDIUS                    It sits too near you.
ANTONY
Here, here it lies, a lump of lead by day,
And, in my short distracted nightly slumbers,                    280
The hag that rides my dreams.—
VENTIDIUS
Out with it; give it vent.
ANTONY                         Urge not my shame.
I lost a battle.
VENTIDIUS        So has Julius done.
ANTONY
Thou favour'st me, and speak'st not half thou think'st;
For Julius fought it out, and lost it fairly:                    285
But Antony—
VENTIDIUS        Nay, stop not.
ANTONY                           Antony—
Well, thou wilt have it—like a coward fled,
Fled while his soldiers fought; fled first, Ventidius.
Thou long'st to curse me, and I give thee leave.
I know thou cam'st prepared to rail.
VENTIDIUS                              I did.                     290
ANTONY
I'll help thee—I have been a man, Ventidius—
VENTIDIUS
Yes, and a brave one; but—
ANTONY                       I know thy meaning:
But I have lost my reason, have disgraced
The name of soldier with inglorious ease;
In the full vintage of my flowing honours,                      295
Sat still, and saw it pressed by other hands.
Fortune came smiling to my youth, and wooed it,

290 *cam'st* Q1, W2 (com'st Q2, Q3, W1)

---

286–90 *Antony ... rail* cf. Sedley, *Antony and Cleopatra*, I. ii, 57–61:
    The just reproach has roused my lion heart,
    Nor am I angry at the friendly smart.
    I fled, Canidius, basely ran away,
    And fought for Empire below those for pay.
    Of my new shame too much thou canst not say.

And purple greatness met my ripened years.
When first I came to empire, I was borne
On tides of people crowding to my triumphs—                300
The wish of nations! And the willing world
Received me as its pledge of future peace:
I was so great, so happy, so beloved,
Fate could not ruin me, till I took pains
And worked against my fortune, chid her from me,           305
And turned her loose; yet still she came again.
My careless days and my luxurious nights
At length have wearied her, and now she's gone,
Gone, gone, divorced forever. Help me, soldier,
To curse this madman, this industrious fool,               310
Who laboured to be wretched: prithee, curse me.
VENTIDIUS
    No.
ANTONY Why?
VENTIDIUS        You are too sensible already
    Of what y'have done, too conscious of your failings,
    And like a scorpion, whipped by others first
    To fury, sting yourself in mad revenge.                315
    I would bring balm, and pour it in your wounds,
    Cure your distempered mind, and heal your fortunes.
ANTONY
    I know thou wouldst.
VENTIDIUS                I will.
ANTONY                            Ha, ha, ha, ha.
VENTIDIUS
    You laugh.
ANTONY        I do, to see officious love
    Give cordials to the dead.
VENTIDIUS                        You would be lost, then?     320
ANTONY
    I am.
VENTIDIUS I say you are not. Try your fortune.
ANTONY
    I have, to th'utmost. Dost thou think me desperate
    Without just cause? No, when I found all lost
    Beyond repair, I hid me from the world,
    And learnt to scorn it here; which now I do              325
    So heartily, I think it is not worth
    The cost of keeping.

298 *purple greatness* Antony wore the *trabea*, the purple cloak of state.

VENTIDIUS                Caesar thinks not so:
  He'll thank you for the gift he could not take.
  You would be killed like Tully, would you? Do,
  Hold out your throat to Caesar, and die tamely.      330
ANTONY
  No, I can kill myself; and so resolve.
VENTIDIUS
  I can die with you, too, when time shall serve;
  But Fortune calls upon us now to live,
  To fight, to conquer.
ANTONY                Sure thou dream'st, Ventidius.
VENTIDIUS
  No, 'tis you dream; you sleep away your hours      335
  In desperate sloth, miscalled philosophy.
  Up, up, for honour's sake: twelve legions wait you,
  And long to call you chief; by painful journeys
  I led 'em, patient both of heat and hunger,
  Down from the Parthian marches to the Nile.      340
  'Twill do you good to see their sunburnt faces,
  Their scarred cheeks, and chopped hands; there's virtue in
                                        'em:
  They'll sell those mangled limbs at dearer rates
  Than yon trim bands can buy.
ANTONY                Where left you them?
VENTIDIUS
  I said in Lower Syria.
ANTONY                Bring 'em hither;      345
  There may be life in these.
VENTIDIUS                They will not come.
ANTONY
  Why didst thou mock my hopes with promised aids
  To double my despair? They're mutinous.
VENTIDIUS
  Most firm and loyal.
ANTONY                Yet they will not march
  To succour me. O trifler!
VENTIDIUS                They petition      350
  You would make haste to head 'em.
ANTONY                I'm besieged.

---

329 *Tully* Marcus Tullius Cicero (106–43 B.C.) was nominated for
    proscription by Antony. According to Plutarch, he tried to flee from
    those sent to kill him, but on being overtaken, stretched his head out of
    the litter in which he was travelling to facilitate his execution.

C

VENTIDIUS
  There's but one way shut up: how came I hither?
ANTONY
  I will not stir.
VENTIDIUS          They would perhaps desire
  A better reason.
ANTONY                I have never used
  My soldiers to demand a reason of                            355
  My actions. Why did they refuse to march?
VENTIDIUS
  They said they would not fight for Cleopatra.
ANTONY
  What was't they said?
VENTIDIUS
  They said they would not fight for Cleopatra.
  Why should they fight, indeed, to make her conquer,          360
  And make you more a slave? To gain your kingdoms,
  Which, for a kiss at your next midnight feast,
  You'll sell to her? Then she new names her jewels,
  And calls this diamond such or such a tax;
  Each pendant in her ear shall be a province.                 365
ANTONY
  Ventidius, I allow your tongue free licence
  On all my other faults; but, on your life,
  No word of Cleopatra: she deserves
  More worlds than I can lose.
VENTIDIUS                            Behold, you Powers,
  To whom you have intrusted humankind:                        370
  See Europe, Afric, Asia put in balance,
  And all weighed down by one light, worthless woman!
  I think the gods are Antonies, and give,
  Like prodigals, this nether world away
  To none but wasteful hands.

353–6 *They would ... actions* cf. Sedley, *Antony and Cleopatra*, I. ii, 128–31:
  MEMNON
    'Tis ill to discontent whom we must use,
    And men fight best when they their party choose.
  ANTONY
    'Tis chosen for 'em by their Sovereign,
    And 'tis sedition in them to complain.
  Sedley, unlike Dryden, depicts Antony's position as changing: when the
  army and citizens revolt at his tyranny, he says: '... just Heaven, what
  am I,/Whom the rude people teach humanity?' (III. ii, 331–2).

ANTONY You grow presumptuous. 375
VENTIDIUS
I take the privilege of plain love to speak.
ANTONY
Plain love? Plain arrogance, plain insolence!
Thy men are cowards, thou an envious traitor,
Who, under seeming honesty, hast vented
The burden of thy rank, o'erflowing gall. 380
Oh, that thou wert my equal, great in arms
As the first Caesar was, that I might kill thee
Without a stain to honour!
VENTIDIUS You may kill me;
You have done more already: called me traitor.
ANTONY
Art thou not one?
VENTIDIUS For showing you yourself, 385
Which none else durst have done. But had I been
That name, which I disdain to speak again,
I needed not have sought your abject fortunes,
Come to partake your fate, to die with you:
What hindered me t'have led my conquering eagles 390
To fill Octavius' bands? I could have been
A traitor then, a glorious, happy traitor,
And not have been so called.
ANTONY Forgive me, soldier:
I've been too passionate.
VENTIDIUS You thought me false,
Thought my old age betrayed you: kill me, Sir, 395
Pray, kill me; yet you need not; your unkindness
Has left your sword no work.
ANTONY I did not think so;
I said it in my rage; prithee forgive me.
Why didst thou tempt my anger by discovery
Of what I would not hear?
VENTIDIUS No prince but you 400
Could merit that sincerity I used,
Nor durst another man have ventured it:
But you, ere love misled your wandering eyes,
Were sure the chief and best of human race,
Framed in the very pride and boast of Nature, 405
So perfect that the gods who formed you wondered
At their own skill, and cried, 'A lucky hit
Has mended our design'. Their envy hindered,
Else you had been immortal, and a pattern,
When Heaven would work for ostentation sake, 410

To copy out again.
ANTONY         But Cleopatra—
Go on, for I can bear it now.
VENTIDIUS                    No more.
ANTONY
Thou dar'st not trust my passion, but thou mayst:
Thou only lov'st, the rest have flattered me.
VENTIDIUS
Heaven's blessing on your heart for that kind word.     415
May I believe you love me? Speak again.
ANTONY
Indeed I do. Speak this, and this, and this.   (*Hugging him*)
Thy praises were unjust, but I'll deserve 'em,
And yet mend all. Do with me what thou wilt;
Lead me to victory: thou know'st the way.     420
VENTIDIUS
And will you leave this—
ANTONY                    Prithee, do not curse her,
And I will leave her; though, Heaven knows, I love
Beyond life, conquest, empire, all but honour;
But I will leave her.
VENTIDIUS          That's my royal master.
And shall we fight?
ANTONY              I warrant thee, old soldier,     425
Thou shalt behold me once again in iron,
And at the head of our old troops that beat
The Parthians cry aloud, 'Come, follow me'.
VENTIDIUS
Oh, now I hear my Emperor! In that word
Octavius fell. Gods, let me see that day,     430
And if I have ten years behind, take all;
I'll thank you for th'exchange.
ANTONY                        Oh Cleopatra!
VENTIDIUS
Again?
ANTONY I've done. In that last sigh she went.
Caesar shall know what 'tis to force a lover
From all he holds most dear.
VENTIDIUS                    Methinks you breathe     435
Another soul: your looks are more divine;
You speak a hero, and you move a god.
ANTONY
Oh, thou hast fired me; my soul's up in arms,
And mans each part about me: once again
That noble eagerness of fight has seized me,     440

That eagerness with which I darted upward
To Cassius' camp; in vain the steepy hill
Opposed my way, in vain a war of spears
Sung round my head, and planted all my shield:
I won the trenches while my foremost men                445
Lagged on the plain below.
VENTIDIUS                    Ye gods, ye gods,
For such another hour.
ANTONY                    Come on, my soldier!
Our hearts and arms are still the same: I long
Once more to meet our foes, that thou and I,
Like Time and Death, marching before our troops,      450
May taste fate to 'em; mow 'em out a passage,
   And entering where the foremost squadrons yield,
   Begin the noble harvest of the field.          (*Exeunt*)

## Act II

*Enter* CLEOPATRA, IRAS, *and* ALEXAS

CLEOPATRA
What shall I do, or whither shall I turn?
Ventidius has o'ercome, and he will go.
ALEXAS
He goes to fight for you.
CLEOPATRA
Then he would see me ere he went to fight.
Flatter me not: if once he goes, he's lost,            5
And all my hopes destroyed.
ALEXAS                    Does this weak passion
Become a mighty queen?
CLEOPATRA                    I am no queen:
Is this to be a queen, to be besieged
By yon insulting Roman, and to wait
Each hour the victor's chain? These ills are small;   10
For Antony is lost, and I can mourn

447 *hour* Q1, Q2, W2 (honour Q3, W1)
   s.d. *Enter* Q3, W1 (om. Q1, Q2, W2)

441–6 *That eagerness . . . below* See Introduction, p. xiv.

For nothing else but him. Now come, Octavius,
I have no more to lose; prepare thy bands;
I'm fit to be a captive: Antony
Has taught my mind the fortune of a slave.                    15
IRAS
Call reason to assist you.
CLEOPATRA                    I have none,
And none would have. My love's a noble madness,
Which shows the cause deserved it. Moderate sorrow
Fits vulgar love, and for a vulgar man;
But I have loved with such transcendent passion,            20
I soared at first quite out of reason's view,
And now am lost above it. No, I'm proud
'Tis thus: would Antony could see me now;
Think you he would not sigh? Though he must leave me,
Sure he would sigh, for he is noble-natured,                25
And bears a tender heart: I know him well.
Ah, no, I know him not: I knew him once,
But now 'tis past.
IRAS                    Let it be past with you:
Forget him, Madam.
CLEOPATRA                Never, never, Iras.
He once was mine; and once, though now 'tis gone,          30
Leaves a faint image of possession still.
ALEXAS
Think him unconstant, cruel, and ungrateful.
CLEOPATRA
I cannot: if I could, those thoughts were vain;
Faithless, ungrateful, cruel though he be,
I still must love him.

*Enter* CHARMION

                    Now, what news, my Charmion?          35
Will he be kind, and will he not forsake me?
Am I to live, or die? Nay, do I live,
Or am I dead? For when he gave his answer,
Fate took the word, and then I lived or died.
CHARMION
I found him, Madam—
CLEOPATRA                    A long speech preparing?      40

30–1 *He once . . . still* The section of Lucretius' *De Rerum Natura* quoted
    by Dryden (Preface, ll. 273–4) also includes a line, 'If absent, her idea
    still appears' (Dryden's translation, l. 15).

If thou bring'st comfort, haste, and give it me,
For never was more need.
IRAS                                    I know he loves you.
CLEOPATRA
Had he been kind, her eyes had told me so
Before her tongue could speak it: now she studies
To soften what he said; but give me death                    45
Just as he sent it, Charmion, undisguised,
And in the words he spoke.
CHARMION                        I found him, then,
Encompassed round, I think, with iron statues,
So mute, so motionless his soldiers stood,
While awfully he cast his eyes about,                        50
And every leader's hopes or fears surveyed.
Methought he looked resolved, and yet not pleased.
When he beheld me struggling in the crowd,
He blushed, and bade make way.
ALEXAS                             There's comfort yet.
CHARMION
Ventidius fixed his eyes upon my passage                     55
Severely, as he meant to frown me back,
And sullenly gave place: I told my message
Just as you gave it, broken and disordered.
I numbered in it all your sighs and tears,
And while I moved your pitiful request,                      60
That you but only begged a last farewell,
He fetched an inward groan, and every time
I named you, sighed as if his heart were breaking,
But shunned my eyes, and guiltily looked down:
He seemed not now that awful Antony                          65
Who shook an armed assembly with his nod,
But making show as he would rub his eyes,
Disguised and blotted out a falling tear.
CLEOPATRA
Did he then weep, and was I worth a tear?
If what thou hast to say be not as pleasing,                 70
Tell me no more, but let me die contented.
CHARMION
He bid me say, he knew himself so well,
He could deny you nothing if he saw you,
And therefore—
CLEOPATRA          Thou wouldst say, he would not see me?
CHARMION
And therefore begged you not to use a power                  75
Which he could ill resist; yet he should ever

Respect you as he 'ought.
CLEOPATRA            Is that a word
For Antony to use to Cleopatra?
Oh that faint word, 'respect'! How I disdain it!
Disdain myself, for loving after it!                                80
He should have kept that word for cold Octavia.
Respect is for a wife: am I that thing,
That dull, insipid lump, without desires,
And without power to give 'em?
ALEXAS                        You misjudge:
You see through love, and that deludes your sight             85
As what is straight seems crooked through the water;
But I, who bear my reason undisturbed,
Can see this Antony, this dreaded man,
A fearful slave who fain would run away,
And shuns his master's eyes. If you pursue him,             90
My life on't, he still drags a chain along,
That needs must clog his flight.
CLEOPATRA                  Could I believe thee!—
ALEXAS
By every circumstance I know he loves.
True, he's hard pressed by interest and by honour;
Yet he but doubts, and parleys, and casts out             95
Many a long look for succour.
CLEOPATRA                  He sends word
He fears to see my face.
ALEXAS                  And would you more?
He shows his weakness who declines the combat,
And you must urge your fortune. Could he speak
More plainly? To my ears the message sounds:             100
'Come to my rescue, Cleopatra, come;
Come, free me from Ventidius, from my tyrant:
See me, and give me a pretence to leave him'.
I hear his trumpets. This way he must pass.

96 *look* Q1, W2 (looked Q2, Q3, W1)

---

82–4 *Respect . . . 'em* In Dryden's *Aureng-Zebe* (1675; published 1676), the
villainous Nourmahal justifies her incestuous love by saying: 'Love
sure's a name that's more divine than wife' (III, 367–9).
86–7 *what . . . undisturbed* Sceptics used the example of a straight stick's
appearing to be crooked in water as part of their attack on the use of
sensory data to formulate rationalist dogma (Louis Bredvold, *The Intellectual Milieu of John Dryden*, 1934, reprint Ann Arbor, 1966, pp.
18–19).

Please you, retire a while; I'll work him first,                    105
That he may bend more easy.
CLEOPATRA                    You shall rule me;
But all, I fear, in vain.
                    (*Exit with* CHARMION *and* IRAS)
ALEXAS                    I fear so too,
Though I concealed my thoughts to make her bold;
But 'tis our utmost means, and Fate befriend it.
                    (*Withdraws*)


*Enter lictors with fasces, one bearing the eagle; then enter*
ANTONY *with* VENTIDIUS, *followed by other commanders*


ANTONY
Octavius is the minion of blind chance,                    110
But holds from virtue nothing.
VENTIDIUS                    Has he courage?
ANTONY
But just enough to season him from coward.
Oh, 'tis the coldest youth upon a charge,
The most deliberate fighter! If he ventures
(As in Illyria once they say he did,                    115
To storm a town), 'tis when he cannot choose,
When all the world have fixed their eyes upon him;
And then he lives on that for seven years after:
But at a close revenge he never fails.
VENTIDIUS
I heard you challenged him.
ANTONY                    I did, Ventidius.                    120
What think'st thou was his answer? 'Twas so tame:


105–6 *I'll . . . easy* cf. *Julius Caesar*, II. i, 209–10: 'Let me work;/For I can
    give his humour the true bent,/And I will bring him to the Capitol'
    (Klima).
109 s.d. *lictors with fasces* The *fasces*, a bundle of rods and an axe, were
    carried by attendants before dignitaries. The *eagle* was the principal
    standard of a Roman legion.
110 *minion . . . chance* cf. Shakespeare, *Antony and Cleopatra*, II. iii, 34–6:
    'The very dice obey him;/And in our sports my better cunning faints/
    Under his chance'.
111 *holds . . . nothing* See Preface, ll. 156–9.
112 *coward* traditionally assumed to be an attack on Louis XIV (Vieth,
    op. cit., p. 54).

He said he had more ways than one to die;
I had not.
VENTIDIUS   Poor!
ANTONY          He has more ways than one,
But he would choose 'em all before that one.
VENTIDIUS
He first would choose an ague or a fever.                    125
ANTONY
No, it must be an ague, not a fever:
He has not warmth enough to die by that.
VENTIDIUS
Or old age and a bed.
ANTONY                  Ay, there's his choice.
He would live, like a lamp, to the last wink,
And crawl upon the utmost verge of life.                    130
Oh Hercules! Why should a man like this,
Who dares not trust his fate for one great action,
Be all the care of Heaven? Why should he lord it
O'er fourscore thousand men, of whom each one
Is braver than himself?
VENTIDIUS                You conquered for him:          135
Philippi knows it; there you shared with him
That empire which your sword made all your own.
ANTONY
Fool that I was, upon my eagle's wings
I bore this wren till I was tired with soaring,
And now he mounts above me.                                140
Good heavens, is this, is this the man who braves me?
Who bids my age make way, drives me before him
To the world's ridge and sweeps me off like rubbish?

122 *one* Q1, Q2, W2 (om. Q3, W1)

---

122–3 *He said . . . not* cf. Shakespeare, *Antony and Cleopatra*, IV. i, 5: 'I
    have many other ways to die'. Dryden follows Shakespeare's use of
    North's mistranslation of Plutarch.
131 *Hercules* Plutarch says that Antony traced his ancestry back to Hercules,
    and compares Antony under Cleopatra's spell to Hercules stripped of his
    lionskin and club by Omphale. See also II, 206; II, 393; III, 13; III,
    41–2; IV, 60.
139 *wren . . . soaring* a reference to the fable of a wren which rode on the
    back of an eagle (the symbol of the Roman army) until the eagle was
    weary, and then took wing and soared above it.

VENTIDIUS
  Sir, we lose time; the troops are mounted all.
ANTONY
  Then give the word to march.                    145
  I long to leave this prison of a town,
  To join thy legions, and in open field
  Once more to show my face. Lead, my deliverer.


                    *Enter* ALEXAS


ALEXAS
  Great Emperor,
  In mighty arms renowned above mankind,          150
  But, in soft pity to th'oppressed, a god,
  This message sends the mournful Cleopatra
  To her departing lord.
VENTIDIUS                    Smooth sycophant!
ALEXAS
  A thousand wishes and ten thousand prayers,
  Millions of blessings wait you to the wars.     155
  Millions of sighs and tears she sends you too,
  And would have sent
  As many dear embraces to your arms,
  As many parting kisses to your lips,
  But those, she fears, have wearied you already. 160
VENTIDIUS *aside*
  False crocodile!
ALEXAS
  And yet she begs not now you would not leave her.
  That were a wish too mighty for her hopes,
  Too presuming
  For her low fortune, and your ebbing love;      165
  That were a wish for her more prosperous days,
  Her blooming beauty, and your growing kindness.
ANTONY *aside*
  Well, I must man it out: what would the Queen?
ALEXAS
  First, to these noble warriors who attend


153 *sycophant!* Q1, Q2, W2 (sycophant? Q3, W1)
164–5 *Too . . . love* ed. (1 line in Q1)

Your daring courage in the chase of fame—                     170
Too daring and too dangerous for her quiet—
She humbly recommends all she holds dear,
All her own cares and fears: the care of you.
VENTIDIUS
Yes, witness Actium.
ANTONY                    Let him speak, Ventidius.
ALEXAS
You, when his matchless valour bears him forward        175
With ardour too heroic on his foes,
Fall down, as she would do, before his feet;
Lie in his way, and stop the paths of death:
Tell him this god is not invulnerable,
That absent Cleopatra bleeds in him;                          180
And, that you may remember her petition,
She begs you wear these trifles as a pawn
Which, at your wished return, she will redeem
                    (*Gives jewels to the commanders*)
With all the wealth of Egypt.
This to the great Ventidius she presents,                     185
Whom she can never count her enemy,
Because he loves her lord.
VENTIDIUS                    Tell her I'll none on't:
I'm not ashamed of honest poverty.
Not all the diamonds of the East can bribe
Ventidius from his faith. I hope to see                       190
These, and the rest of all her sparkling store,
Where they shall more deservingly be placed.
ANTONY
And who must wear 'em then?
VENTIDIUS                    The wronged Octavia.
ANTONY
You might have spared that word.
VENTIDIUS                    And he that bribe.
ANTONY
But have I no remembrance?
ALEXAS                    Yes, a dear one:                    195
Your slave, the Queen—
ANTONY                    My mistress.
ALEXAS                    Then your mistress.
Your mistress would, she says, have sent her soul,
But that you had long since. She humbly begs
This ruby bracelet, set with bleeding hearts,
The emblems of her own, may bind your arm.                    200
                    (*Presenting a bracelet*)

VENTIDIUS
Now, my best Lord, in honour's name I ask you,
For manhood's sake, and for your own dear safety,
Touch not these poisoned gifts,
Infected by the sender; touch 'em not.
Myriads of bluest plagues lie underneath 'em,                    205
And more than aconite has dipped the silk.

ANTONY
Nay, now you grow too cynical, Ventidius:
A lady's favours may be worn with honour.
What, to refuse her bracelet! On my soul,
When I lie pensive in my tent alone,                             210
'Twill pass the wakeful hours of winter nights
To tell these pretty beads upon my arm,
To count for every one a soft embrace,
A melting kiss at such and such a time,
And now and then the fury of her love                           215
When—and what harm's in this?

ALEXAS                              None, none my Lord,
But what's to her, that now 'tis past forever.

ANTONY *going to tie it*
We soldiers are so awkward—help me tie it.

ALEXAS
In faith, my Lord, we courtiers too are awkward
In these affairs. So are all men indeed;                        220
Even I, who am not one. But shall I speak?

ANTONY
Yes, freely.

ALEXAS          Then, my Lord, fair hands alone
Are fit to tie it: she who sent it can.

206 *aconite* the poison derived from the plant of the same name; it has a
numbing effect when applied externally. In the Hercules legend,
Deianeira, his wife, had her jealousy aroused by learning that Hercules'
long absence fighting a war was motivated by his desire to win Iole,
although this meant destroying her country. She anointed a robe with
the blood of Nessus, a centaur killed by Hercules, with an arrow dipped
in the blood of the Lernean Hydra, for attempting to rape her, as the
dying Nessus had told her it would act as a love potion. In fact it destroyed Hercules, who after prolonged torment was taken up to
Olympus by the gods. Deianeira, on finding that the half-man had
deceived her, killed herself.

219–20 *In faith ... indeed* cf. Shakespeare, *Antony and Cleopatra*, IV. iv,
14–15: 'Thou fumblest, Eros, and my queen's a squire/More tight at this
than thou'.

VENTIDIUS
 Hell, death! this eunuch pander ruins you.
 You will not see her?
     (ALEXAS *whispers an attendant, who goes out*)
ANTONY     But to take my leave.    225
VENTIDIUS
 Then I have washed an Ethiope. Y'are undone;
 Y'are in the toils; y'are taken; y'are destroyed:
 Her eyes do Caesar's work.
ANTONY     You fear too soon.
 I'm constant to myself, I know my strength;
 And yet she shall not think me barbarous neither,  230
 Born in the depths of Afric. I'm a Roman,
 Bred to the rules of soft humanity.
 A guest, and kindly used, should bid farewell.
VENTIDIUS
 You do not know
 How weak you are to her, how much an infant;  235
 You are not proof against a smile or glance;
 A sigh will quite disarm you.
ANTONY     See, she comes!
 Now you shall find your error. Gods, I thank you:
 I formed the danger greater than it was,
 And now 'tis near, 'tis lessened.
VENTIDIUS     Mark the end yet.   240

*Enter* CLEOPATRA, CHARMION, *and* IRAS

ANTONY
 Well, Madam, we are met.
CLEOPATRA     Is this a meeting?
 Then we must part?
ANTONY    We must.
CLEOPATRA     Who says we must?
ANTONY
 Our own hard fates.
CLEOPATRA    We make those fates ourselves.

---

226 *washed an Ethiope* undertaken an impossible task of redemption (pro-
  verbial).
230 *barbarous* cf. Sedley, *Antony and Cleopatra*, III. ii, 58–9: 'I could not . . .
  my best queen so barbarously quit'.

ANTONY
    Yes, we have made 'em; we have loved each other
    Into our mutual ruin.                                    245
CLEOPATRA
    The gods have seen my joys with envious eyes;
    I have no friends in Heaven, and all the world,
    As 'twere the business of mankind to part us,
    Is armed against my love: even you yourself
    Join with the rest; you, you are armed against me.        250
ANTONY
    I will be justified in all I do
    To late posterity, and therefore hear me.
    If I mix a lie
    With any truth, reproach me freely with it;
    Else favour me with silence.
CLEOPATRA                   You command me,        255
    And I am dumb.
VENTIDIUS
    I like this well: he shows authority.
ANTONY
    That I derive my ruin
    From you alone—
CLEOPATRA         O Heavens! I ruin you?
ANTONY
    You promised me your silence, and you break it        260
    Ere I have scarce begun.
CLEOPATRA             Well, I obey you.
ANTONY
    When I beheld you first, it was in Egypt,
    Ere Caesar saw your eyes. You gave me love,
    And were too young to know it: that I settled
    Your father in his throne was for your sake;        265
    I left th'acknowledgement for time to ripen.
    Caesar stepped in, and with a greedy hand
    Plucked the green fruit ere the first blush of red,
    Yet cleaving to the bough. He was my lord,
    And was, beside, too great for me to rival,        270
    But I deserved you first, though he enjoyed you.

245 *Into* Q1, Q2, Q3, W2 (In W1)
263 *eyes. You* ed. (eyes; you Q1, Q2, W2 eyes, you Q3, W1)

---

253–5 *If I . . . silence* See Introduction, p. xxv.
267–9 *Caesar . . . bough* cf. Shakespeare, *Antony and Cleopatra*, I. v, 73–5:
    'My salad days,/When I was green in judgement, cold in blood'.

When, after, I beheld you in Cilicia,
An enemy to Rome, I pardoned you.
CLEOPATRA
I cleared myself—
ANTONY                 Again you break your promise.
I loved you still, and took your weak excuses,                    275
Took you into my bosom, stained by Caesar,
And not half mine. I went to Egypt with you,
And hid me from the business of the world,
Shut out enquiring nations from my sight,
To give whole years to you.                                      280
VENTIDIUS *aside*
Yes, to your shame be't spoken.
ANTONY                           How I loved,
Witness ye days and nights, and all your hours
That danced away with down upon your feet,
As all your business were to count my passion.
One day passed by, and nothing saw but love;                     285
Another came, and still 'twas only love:
The suns were wearied out with looking on,
And I untired with loving.
I saw you every day, and all the day,
And every day was still but as the first,                        290
So eager was I still to see you more.
VENTIDIUS
'Tis all too true.
ANTONY                 Fulvia, my wife, grew jealous,
As she indeed had reason; raised a war
In Italy, to call me back.
VENTIDIUS                   But yet
You went not.
ANTONY           While within your arms I lay,                   295
The world fell mouldering from my hands each hour,
And left me scarce a grasp: I thank your love for't.
VENTIDIUS
Well pushed: that last was home.
CLEOPATRA                           Yet may I speak?
ANTONY
If I have urged a falsehood, yes; else, not.

---

281–3 *How . . . feet* cf. Shakespeare, *Antony and Cleopatra*, I. i, 44–5: 'Now
    for the love of Love and her soft hours,/Let's not confound the time with
    conference harsh'.
292 *Fulvia* See Introduction, p. xiv.

Your silence says I have not. Fulvia died— 300
Pardon, you gods, with my unkindness died.
To set the world at peace I took Octavia,
This Caesar's sister: in her pride of youth
And flower of beauty did I wed that lady,
Whom blushing I must praise, because I left her. 305
You called; my love obeyed the fatal summons:
This raised the Roman arms; the cause was yours.
I would have fought by land, where I was stronger;
You hindered it, yet when I fought at sea,
Forsook me fighting, and—oh, stain to honour! 310
Oh, lasting shame!—I knew not that I fled,
But fled to follow you.

VENTIDIUS
What haste she made to hoist her purple sails!
And, to appear magnificent in flight,
Drew half our strength away.

ANTONY                              All this you caused, 315
And would you multiply more ruins on me?
This honest man, my best, my only friend,
Has gathered up the shipwreck of my fortunes.
Twelve legions I have left, my last recruits,
And you have watched the news, and bring your eyes 320
To seize them too. If you have aught to answer,
Now speak, you have free leave.

ALEXAS *aside*                        She stands confounded.
Despair is in her eyes.

VENTIDIUS
Now lay a sigh i'th'way to stop his passage;
Prepare a tear, and bid it for his legions: 325
'Tis like they shall be sold.

CLEOPATRA
How shall I plead my cause, when you, my judge,
Already have condemned me? Shall I bring
The love you bore me for my advocate?
That now is turned against me, that destroys me, 330
For love once past is at the best forgotten,
But oftener sours to hate: 'twill please my Lord
To ruin me, and therefore I'll be guilty.
But could I once have thought it would have pleased you,
That you would pry with narrow searching eyes 335
Into my faults, severe to my destruction,
And watching all advantages with care
That serve to make me wretched? Speak, my Lord,
For I end here. Though I deserve this usage,

    Was it like you to give it?

ANTONY                Oh, you wrong me      340
  To think I sought this parting, or desired
  To accuse you more than what will clear myself
  And justify this breach.

CLEOPATRA       Thus low I thank you,
  And since my innocence will not offend,
  I shall not blush to own it.

VENTIDIUS           After this,      345
  I think she'll blush at nothing.

CLEOPATRA          You seem grieved
  (And therein you are kind), that Caesar first
  Enjoyed my love, though you deserved it better:
  I grieve for that, my Lord, much more than you,
  For had I first been yours, it would have saved      350
  My second choice; I never had been his,
  And ne'er had been but yours. But Caesar first,
  You say, possessed my love. Not so, my Lord:
  He first possessed my person, you my love;
  Caesar loved me, but I loved Antony.      355
  If I endured him after, 'twas because
  I judged it due to the first name of men,
  And, half constrained, I gave, as to a tyrant,
  What he would take by force.

VENTIDIUS         O siren! Siren!
  Yet grant that all the love she boasts were true,      360
  Has she not ruined you? I still urge that,
  The fatal consequence.

CLEOPATRA       The consequence indeed,
  For I dare challenge him, my greatest foe,
  To say it was designed: 'tis true I loved you,
  And kept you far from an uneasy wife:      365
  Such Fulvia was.
  Yes, but he'll say you left Octavia for me;—
  And can you blame me to receive that love
  Which quitted such desert for worthless me?
  How often have I wished some other Caesar,      370
  Great as the first, and as the second young,
  Would court my love, to be refused for you!

VENTIDIUS
  Words, words; but Actium, Sir, remember Actium.

---

341 *or* Q1, Q2, Q3, W2 (as W1)
365 *wife* Q1, Q2, W2 (will Q3, W1)

CLEOPATRA

Even there I dare his malice. True, I counselled
To fight at sea, but I betrayed you not.                      375
I fled, but not to the enemy. 'Twas fear:
Would I had been a man, not to have feared,
For none would then have envied me your friendship,
Who envy me your love.

ANTONY                    We're both unhappy.
If nothing else, yet our ill fortune parts us.              380
Speak: would you have me perish by my stay?

CLEOPATRA

If as a friend you ask my judgement, go;
If as a lover, stay. If you must perish—
'Tis a hard word—but stay.

VENTIDIUS

See now th'effects of her so boasted love!                  385
She strives to drag you down to ruin with her;
But could she 'scape without you, oh, how soon
Would she let go her hold, and haste to shore,
And never look behind!

CLEOPATRA

Then judge my love by this.    (*Giving* ANTONY *a writing*)
                        Could I have borne            390
A life or death, a happiness or woe
From yours divided, this had given me means.

ANTONY

By Hercules, the writing of Octavius!
I know it well; 'tis that proscribing hand,
Young as it was, that led the way to mine,                  395
And left me but the second place in murder.—
See, see, Ventidius! Here he offers Egypt,
And joins all Syria to it as a present,
So, in requital, she forsake my fortunes,
And join her arms with his.

CLEOPATRA                    And yet you leave me!          400
You leave me, Antony, and yet I love you,
Indeed I do. I have refused a kingdom;
That's a trifle:
For I could part with life, with anything

---

382–4 *If as . . . stay* cf. Sedley, *Antony and Cleopatra*, I. ii, 265–6: 'I know as
    well as you 'tis fit you go,/Yet what is best I cannot let you do'.
394 *proscribing* The triumvirate (Antony, Octavius, and Lepidus) put to
    death many of their political opponents. See *Julius Caesar*, IV. i.

But only you. Oh, let me die but with you!          405
Is that a hard request?
ANTONY                    Next living with you,
'Tis all that Heaven can give.
ALEXAS *aside*                    He melts; we conquer.
CLEOPATRA
No; you shall go. Your interest calls you hence;
Yes, your dear interest pulls too strong for these
Weak arms to hold you here.—          (*Takes his hand*)
                    Go, leave me, soldier,          410
For you're no more a lover, leave me dying:
Push me all pale and panting from your bosom,
And when your march begins, let one run after,
Breathless almost for joy, and cry, 'She's dead'.
The soldiers shout; you then perhaps may sigh,          415
And muster all your Roman gravity.
Ventidius chides, and straight your brow clears up,
As I had never been.
ANTONY                    Gods, 'tis too much,
Too much for man to bear!
CLEOPATRA                    What is't for me, then,
A weak, forsaken woman, and a lover?—          420
Here let me breathe my last: envy me not
This minute in your arms; I'll die apace,
As fast as e'er I can, and end your trouble.
ANTONY
Die? Rather let me perish! Loosened Nature
Leap from its hinges; sink the props of Heaven,          425
And fall the skies to crush the nether world!
My eyes, my soul, my all!—          (*Embraces her*)
VENTIDIUS                    And what's this toy
In balance with your fortune, honour, fame?
ANTONY
What is't, Ventidius? It outweighs 'em all;
Why, we have more than conquered Caesar now.          430
My Queen's not only innocent, but loves me.
This, this is she who drags me down to ruin!
But could she 'scape without me, with what haste
Would she let slip her hold, and make to shore,

418–19 *Gods . . . bear* ed. (printed as one line in Q1)

---

424–7 *Die . . . all* cf. Shakespeare, *Antony and Cleopatra*, I. i, 33–5: 'Let
    Rome in Tiber melt, and the wide arch/Of the ranged empire fall! Here
    is my space./Kingdoms are clay . . .

And never look behind! 435
Down on thy knees, blasphemer as thou art,
And ask forgiveness of wronged innocence.

VENTIDIUS
I'll rather die than take it. Will you go?

ANTONY
Go? Whither? Go from all that's excellent?
Faith, honour, virtue, all good things forbid 440
That I should go from her who sets my love
Above the price of kingdoms. Give, you gods,
Give to your boy, your Caesar,
This rattle of a globe to play withal,
This gewgaw world, and put him cheaply off: 445
I'll not be pleased with less than Cleopatra.

CLEOPATRA
She's wholly yours. My heart's so full of joy
That I shall do some wild extravagance
Of love in public, and the foolish world,
Which knows not tenderness, will think me mad. 450

VENTIDIUS
O women! Women! Women! All the gods
Have not such power of doing good to man
As you of doing harm. *(Exit)*

ANTONY                    Our men are armed.
Unbar the gate that looks to Caesar's camp.
I would revenge the treachery he meant me, 455
And long security makes conquest easy.
I'm eager to return before I go,
For all the pleasures I have known beat thick
On my remembrance. How I long for night!
  That both the sweets of mutual love may try, 460
  And once triumph o'er Caesar ere we die. *(Exeunt)*

·

447 *She's* W1, W2 (She Q1, Q2, Q3)
461 *ere* Q2, Q3, W1, W2 (om. Q1)

## Act III

*At one door enter* CLEOPATRA, CHARMION, IRAS, *and* ALEXAS,
*a train of Egyptians; at the other,* ANTONY *and Romans.*
*The entrance on both sides is prepared by music, the trumpets*
*first sounding on Antony's part, then answered by timbrels,*
*etc., on Cleopatra's.* CHARMION *and* IRAS *hold a laurel wreath*
*betwixt them. A dance of Egyptians. After the ceremony,*
CLEOPATRA *crowns* ANTONY

ANTONY
I thought how those white arms would fold me in,
And strain me close, and melt me into love;
So pleased with that sweet image, I sprung forwards,
And added all my strength to every blow.
CLEOPATRA
Come to me, come, my soldier, to my arms! 5
You've been too long away from my embraces;
But when I have you fast, and all my own,
With broken murmurs and with amorous sighs
I'll say you were unkind, and punish you,
And mark you red with many an eager kiss. 10
ANTONY
My brighter Venus!
CLEOPATRA                    O my greater Mars!
ANTONY
Thou join'st us well, my love!
Suppose me come from the Phlegraean plains,
Where gasping giants lay, cleft by my sword,
And mountain tops pared off each other blow 15
To bury those I slew. Receive me, goddess!

1–4 *I thought ... blow* cf. Sedley, *Antony and Cleopatra*, I. ii, 165–6:
'Yet overcharged with love I lost the day,/And in my mistress' presence
ran away'. Dryden contradicts Sedley's conventional neo-classical views
on the effeminacy of love by the use of an argument put forward by
Phaedrus in the *Symposium* (Jowett, op. cit., p. 511).

13 *Phlegraean plains* cf. Sedley, *Antony and Cleopatra*, I. ii, 248–9: 'This
storm once past, in peace and love we'll reign,/Like the immortal gods,
the giants slain'. After the defeat of the Titans, Earth brought forward a
race of giants, born in Phlegrae, to challenge the gods, who had been
told by an oracle that the giants could be defeated by a mortal, and it
was for this reason that Hercules was taken up to Mount Olympus.
When the giants were beaten, each was pinned under a volcano.

Let Caesar spread his subtle nets, like Vulcan:
In thy embraces I would be beheld
By Heaven and earth at once,
And make their envy what they meant their sport.          20
Let those who took us blush; I would love on
With awful state, regardless of their frowns,
As their superior god.
There's no satiety of love in thee:
Enjoyed, thou still art new; perpetual spring             25
Is in thy arms; the ripened fruit but falls,
And blossoms rise to fill its empty place,
And I grow rich by giving.

*Enter* VENTIDIUS, *and stands apart*

ALEXAS

Oh, now the danger's past, your general comes.
He joins not in your joys, nor minds your triumphs,       30
But with contracted brows looks frowning on,
As envying your success.

ANTONY

Now, on my soul, he loves me, truly loves me:
He never flattered me in any vice,
But awes me with his virtue. Even this minute             35
Methinks he has a right of chiding me.
Lead to the temple: I'll avoid his presence;
It checks too strong upon me.          (*Exeunt the rest*)
          (*As* ANTONY *is going,* VENTIDIUS *pulls him by the robe*)
VENTIDIUS                          Emperor.

17-20 *Let . . . sport* Vulcan, jealous of the love of his wife, Venus, and Mars
    (to whom Shakespeare, Sedley, and Dryden all compare Antony and
    Cleopatra) trapped them in bed with a net, and called the other gods to
    laugh at them. Mercury commented that nonetheless he would gladly
    change places with Mars (see IV, 52).
24-8 *There's . . . giving* cf. Shakespeare, *Antony and Cleopatra*, II. ii,
    239-42:
        Age cannot wither her, nor custom stale
        Her infinite variety. Other women cloy
        The appetites they feed, but she makes hungry
        Where most she satisfies.
    Sedley, *Antony and Cleopatra*, I. ii, 240-1: 'My heart shall like those
    trees the East does show,/Where blossoms and ripe fruit hang on one
    bough . . .'
38 s.d. *robe* See note to II, 206.

ANTONY *looking back*
  'Tis the old argument; I prithee spare me.
VENTIDIUS
  But this one hearing, Emperor.
ANTONY                              Let go                              40
  My robe, or by my father Hercules—
VENTIDIUS
  By Hercules his father, that's yet greater,
  I bring you somewhat you would wish to know.
ANTONY
  Thou see'st we are observed; attend me here,
  And I'll return.                        (*Exit*)    45
VENTIDIUS
  I'm waning in his favour, yet I love him;
  I love this man who runs to meet his ruin.
  And sure the gods, like me, are fond of him:
  His virtues lie so mingled with his crimes,
  As would confound their choice to punish one    50
  And not reward the other.

                    *Enter* ANTONY

ANTONY                    We can conquer,
  You see, without your aid.
  We have dislodged their troops;
  They look on us at distance, and like curs
  'Scaped from the lion's paws, they bay far off,    55
  And lick their wounds, and faintly threaten war.
  Five thousand Romans with their faces upward
  Lie breathless on the plain.
VENTIDIUS                    'Tis well; and he
  Who lost 'em could have spared ten thousand more.
  Yet if by this advantage you could gain          60
  An easier peace, while Caesar doubts the chance
  Of arms—
ANTONY        Oh, think not on't, Ventidius:
  The boy pursues my ruin, he'll no peace;
  His malice is considerate in advantage;
  Oh, he's the coolest murderer! So staunch,        65
  He kills, and keeps his temper.
VENTIDIUS                    Have you no friend
  In all his army who has power to move him?
  Maecenas or Agrippa might do much.

  42 *Hercules his father* Jupiter.

**ANTONY**
They're both too deep in Caesar's interests.
We'll work it out by dint of sword, or perish. 70
**VENTIDIUS**
Fain I would find some other.
**ANTONY**                              Thank thy love.
Some four or five such victories as this
Will save thy farther pains.
**VENTIDIUS**
Expect no more; Caesar is on his guard:
I know, Sir, you have conquered against odds, 75
But still you draw supplies from one poor town,
And of Egyptians; he has all the world,
And at his back nations come pouring in
To fill the gaps you make. Pray, think again.
**ANTONY**
Why dost thou drive me from myself, to search 80
For foreign aids? To hunt my memory,
And range all o'er a waste and barren place
To find a friend? The wretched have no friends—
Yet I had one, the bravest youth of Rome,
Whom Caesar loves beyond the love of women; 85
He could resolve his mind as fire does wax,
From that hard, rugged image melt him down,
And mould him in what softer form he pleased.
**VENTIDIUS**
Him would I see, that man of all the world;
Just such a one we want.
**ANTONY**                    He loved me too: 90
I was his soul, he lived not but in me.
We were so closed within each other's breasts,
The rivets were not found that joined us first.
That does not reach us yet: we were so mixed
As meeting streams, both to ourselves were lost; 95
We were one mass; we could not give or take
But from the same, for he was I, I he.
**VENTIDIUS** *aside*
He moves as I would wish him.
**ANTONY**                        After this,
I need not tell his name: 'twas Dollabella.

78 *back* Q1, Q2, Q3 (beck W1, W2)

84–97 *Yet ... I he* See Introduction, p. xxvi.

VENTIDIUS
    He's now in Caesar's camp.
ANTONY                              No matter where,          100
    Since he's no longer mine. He took unkindly
    That I forbade him Cleopatra's sight
    Because I feared he loved her. He confessed
    He had a warmth which, for my sake, he stifled;
    For 'twere impossible that two, so one,          105
    Should not have loved the same. When he departed,
    He took no leave, and that confirmed my thoughts.
VENTIDIUS
    It argues that he loved you more than her,
    Else he had stayed; but he perceived you jealous,
    And would not grieve his friend: I know he loves you.          110
ANTONY
    I should have seen him, then, ere now.
VENTIDIUS                              Perhaps
    He has thus long been labouring for your peace.
ANTONY
    Would he were here.
VENTIDIUS              Would you believe he loved you?
    I read your answer in your eyes: you would.
    Not to conceal it longer, he has sent          115
    A messenger from Caesar's camp with letters.
ANTONY
    Let him appear.
VENTIDIUS          I'll bring him instantly.

*Exit* VENTIDIUS, *and re-enters immediately with* DOLLABELLA

ANTONY
    'Tis he himself! Himself, by holy friendship!
                              (*Runs to embrace him*)
    Art thou returned at last, my better half?
    Come, give me all myself! Let me not live,          120
    If the young bridegroom, longing for his night,
    Was ever half so fond.
DOLLABELLA
    I must be silent, for my soul is busy
    About a nobler work: she's new come home,
    Like a long-absent man, and wanders o'er          125

117 s.d. *and* Q1 corrected, Q2, Q3, W1, W2 (om. Q1 uncorrected)
120 *Come ... live* ed. (printed as 2 ll. 'Come ... myself/Let ... live' Q1)

Each room, a stranger to her own, to look
If all be safe.

ANTONY          Thou hast what's left of me:
For I am now so sunk from what I was,
Thou find'st me at my lowest watermark.
The rivers that ran in and raised my fortunes          130
Are all dried up, or take another course:
What I have left is from my native spring;
I've still a heart that swells in scorn of fate,
And lifts me to my banks.

DOLLABELLA
Still you are lord of all the world to me.              135

ANTONY
Why, then I yet am so; for thou art all.
If I had any joy when thou wert absent,
I grudged it to myself; methought I robbed
Thee of thy part. But, oh my Dollabella!
Thou hast beheld me other than I am.                   140
Hast thou not seen my morning chambers filled
With sceptred slaves who waited to salute me,
With eastern monarchs who forgot the sun
To worship my uprising? Menial kings
Ran coursing up and down my palace-yard,               145
Stood silent in my presence, watched my eyes,
And at my least command all started out
Like racers to the goal.

DOLLABELLA                  Slaves to your fortune.

ANTONY
Fortune is Caesar's now; and what am I?

VENTIDIUS
What you have made yourself; I will not flatter.        150

ANTONY
Is this friendly done?

DOLLABELLA
Yes, when his end is so, I must join with him;
Indeed I must, and yet you must not chide:
Why am I else your friend?

---

140 *Thou ... am* cf. Horace, *Odes*, IV, i. 3: 'I am not such as I was [during
the reign of Cinara's love]'. Horace pleads that he is too old to be plagued
by love, but in the last stanza confesses his love for a young boy. Possibly
Dryden intended to imply an element of homosexuality in Dollabella's
relationships: this would explain why Caesar, who is otherwise the
object only of adverse comment, is said to love Dollabella 'beyond the
love of women' (l. 85).

ANTONY                        Take heed, young man,
 How thou upbraid'st my love: the Queen has eyes,  155
 And thou too hast a soul. Canst thou remember
 When, swelled with hatred, thou beheld'st her first,
 As accessary to thy brother's death?

DOLLABELLA
 Spare my remembrance; 'twas a guilty day,
 And still the blush hangs here.

ANTONY                        To clear herself  160
 For sending him no aid, she came from Egypt.
 Her galley down the silver Cydnos rowed,
 The tackling silk, the streamers waved with gold;
 The gentle winds were lodged in purple sails;

---

162–82 *Her . . . voice* cf. Shakespeare *Antony and Cleopatra*, II. ii, 190–222:
ENOBARBUS
 When she first met Mark Antony she pursed up his heart upon the
river of Cydnus . . .
  The barge she sat in, like a burnished throne
  Burned on the water. The poop was beaten gold;
  Purple the sails, and so perfumèd that
  The winds were love-sick with them; the oars were silver,
  Which to the tune of flutes kept stroke, and made
  The water which they beat to follow faster,
  As amorous of their strokes. For her own person,
  It beggared all description. She did lie
  In her pavilion, cloth-of-gold of tissue,
  O'erpicturing that Venus where we see
  The fancy out-work nature. On each side her
  Stood pretty dimpled boys, like smiling Cupids,
  With divers-coloured fans, whose wind did seem
  To glow the delicate cheeks which they did cool,
  And what they undid did . . .
  Her gentlewomen, like the Nereides,
  So many mermaids, tended her i'th'eyes,
  And made their bends adornings. At the helm
  A seeming mermaid steers. The silken tackle
  Swell with the touches of those flower-soft hands
  That yarely frame the office. From the barge
  A strange invisible perfume hits the sense
  Of the adjacent wharfs. The city cast
  Her people out upon her; and Antony,
  Enthroned i'th'market place, did sit alone,
  Whistling to th'air; which, but for vacancy,
  Had gone to gaze on Cleopatra too,
  And made a gap in nature.

Her nymphs, like Nereids, round her couch were placed,      165
Where she, another sea-born Venus, lay.

DOLLABELLA
No more; I would not hear it.

ANTONY                              Oh, you must!
She lay, and leant her cheek upon her hand,
And cast a look so languishingly sweet
As if, secure of all beholders' hearts,                     170
Neglecting she could take 'em. Boys like Cupids
Stood fanning with their painted wings the winds
That played about her face; but if she smiled,
A darting glory seemed to blaze abroad,
That men's desiring eyes were never wearied,                175
But hung upon the object. To soft flutes
The silver oars kept time; and while they played,
The hearing gave new pleasure to the sight,
And both to thought. 'Twas Heaven, or somewhat more;
For she so charmed all hearts, that gazing crowds           180
Stood panting on the shore, and wanted breath
To give their welcome voice.
Then, Dollabella, where was then thy soul?
Was not thy fury quite disarmed with wonder?
Didst thou not shrink behind me from those eyes,            185
And whisper in my ear, 'Oh, tell her not
That I accused her of my brother's death'?

DOLLABELLA
And should my weakness be a plea for yours?
Mine was an age when love might be excused,
When kindly warmth, and when my springing youth            190
Made it a debt to Nature. Yours—

VENTIDIUS                        Speak boldly.
Yours, he would say, in your declining age,
When no more heat was left but what you forced,
When all the sap was needful for the trunk,
When it went down, then you constrained the course,        195
And robbed from Nature to supply desire;
In you, I would not use so harsh a word,
But 'tis plain dotage.

ANTONY              Ha!

DOLLABELLA              'Twas urged too home.
But yet the loss was private that I made;
'Twas but myself I lost: I lost no legions;                 200
I had no world to lose, no people's love.

ANTONY
This from a friend?

DOLLABELLA            Yes, Antony, a true one;
  A friend so tender that each word I speak
  Stabs my own heart before it reach your ear.
  Oh, judge me not less kind because I chide:            205
  To Caesar I excuse you.
ANTONY                  O ye gods!
  Have I then lived to be excused to Caesar?
DOLLABELLA
  As to your equal.
ANTONY            Well, he's but my equal:
  While I wear this, he never shall be more.
DOLLABELLA
  I bring conditions from him.
ANTONY                      Are they noble?            210
  Methinks thou should'st not bring 'em else. Yet he
  Is full of deep dissembling; knows no honour
  Divided from his interest. Fate mistook him,
  For Nature meant him for an usurer:
  He's fit indeed to buy, not conquer, kingdoms.        215
VENTIDIUS
  Then, granting this,
  What power was theirs who wrought so hard a temper
  To honourable terms?
ANTONY
  It was my Dollabella, or some god.
DOLLABELLA
  Nor I, nor yet Maecenas nor Agrippa:                  220
  They were your enemies, and I a friend
  Too weak alone. Yet 'twas a Roman's deed.
ANTONY
  'Twas like a Roman done: show me that man
  Who has preserved my life, my love, my honour;
  Let me but see his face.
VENTIDIUS            That task is mine,                 225
  And, Heaven, thou know'st how pleasing.
                                    (*Exit* VENTIDIUS)
DOLLABELLA                          You'll remember
  To whom you stand obliged?
ANTONY                    When I forget it,

208 ANTONY . . . *equal* Q1, W2 (om. Q2. To rationalize, Q3 and W1 also om.
    speech prefix l. 210)
209 *be* Q2, Q3, W1, W2 (he Q1)

_____

209 *this* presumably Antony's sword.

Be thou unkind, and that's my greatest curse.
My Queen shall thank him too.
DOLLABELLA                    I fear she will not.
ANTONY
But she shall do't—the Queen, my Dollabella!            230
Hast thou not still some grudgings of thy fever?
DOLLABELLA
I would not see her lost.
ANTONY                    When I forsake her,
Leave me, my better stars, for she has truth
Beyond her beauty. Caesar tempted her,
At no less price than kingdoms, to betray me,            235
But she resisted all; and yet thou chid'st me
For loving her too well. Could I do so?
DOLLABELLA
Yes; there's my reason.

*Enter* VENTIDIUS *with* OCTAVIA, *leading Antony's two little*
DAUGHTERS

ANTONY                    Where?—Octavia there!
                              (*Starting back*)
VENTIDIUS
What, is she poison to you? A disease?
Look on her, view her well, and those she brings:            240
Are they all strangers to your eyes? Has Nature
No secret call, no whisper they are yours?
DOLLABELLA
For shame, my Lord, if not for love, receive 'em
With kinder eyes. If you confess a man,
Meet 'em, embrace 'em, bid 'em welcome to you.            245
Your arms should open, even without your knowledge,
To clasp 'em in; your feet should turn to wings
To bear you to 'em; and your eyes dart out
And aim a kiss ere you could reach the lips.
ANTONY
I stood amazed to think how they came hither.            250
VENTIDIUS
I sent for 'em; I brought 'em in, unknown
To Cleopatra's guards.
DOLLABELLA                    Yet are you cold?
OCTAVIA
Thus long I have attended for my welcome,
Which, as a stranger, sure I might expect.
Who am I?

ANTONY          Caesar's sister.
OCTAVIA                          That's unkind!          255
 Had I been nothing more than Caesar's sister,
 Know, I had still remained in Caesar's camp:
 But your Octavia, your much injured wife,
 Though banished from your bed, driven from your house,
 In spite of Caesar's sister, still is yours.          260
 'Tis true, I have a heart disdains your coldness,
 And prompts me not to seek what you should offer;
 But a wife's virtue still surmounts that pride:
 I come to claim you as my own; to show
 My duty first, to ask, nay beg, your kindness:          265
 Your hand, my Lord; 'tis mine, and I will have it.
         (*Taking his hand*)
VENTIDIUS
 Do, take it; thou deserv'st it.
DOLLABELLA                          On my soul,
 And so she does. She's neither too submissive
 Nor yet too haughty; but so just a mean
 Shows, as it ought, a wife and Roman too.          270
ANTONY
 I fear, Octavia, you have begged my life.
OCTAVIA
 Begged it, my Lord?
ANTONY                          Yes, begged it, my ambassadress,
 Poorly and basely begged it of your brother.
OCTAVIA
 Poorly and basely I could never beg,
 Nor could my brother grant.          275
ANTONY
 Shall I, who to my kneeling slave could say
 'Rise up, and be a king', shall I fall down
 And cry, 'Forgive me, Caesar'? Shall I set
 A man, my equal, in the place of Jove,
 As he could give me being? No; that word          280
 'Forgive' would choke me up,
 And die upon my tongue.
DOLLABELLA                          You shall not need it.
ANTONY
 I will not need it. Come, you've all betrayed me—
 My friend too!—to receive some vile conditions.
 My wife has bought me with her prayers and tears,          285
 And now I must become her branded slave:
 In every peevish mood she will upbraid
 The life she gave; if I but look awry,

She cries, 'I'll tell my brother'.
OCTAVIA                           My hard fortune
Subjects me still to your unkind mistakes.                    290
But the conditions I have brought are such
You need not blush to take. I love your honour
Because 'tis mine; it never shall be said
Octavia's husband was her brother's slave.
Sir, you are free, free even from her you loathe.            295
For though my brother bargains for your love,
Makes me the price and cement of your peace,
I have a soul like yours; I cannot take
Your love as alms, nor beg what I deserve.
I'll tell my brother we are reconciled;                      300
He shall draw back his troops, and you shall march
To rule the East: I may be dropped at Athens—
No matter where, I never will complain,
But only keep the barren name of wife,
And rid you of the trouble.                                  305
VENTIDIUS
Was ever such a strife of sullen honour!
Both scorn to be obliged.
DOLLABELLA
Oh, she has touched him in the tender'st part;
See how he reddens with despite and shame,
To be outdone in generosity!                                 310
VENTIDIUS
See how he winks! How he dries up a tear
That fain would fall!
ANTONY
Octavia, I have heard you, and must praise
The greatness of your soul,
But cannot yield to what you have proposed;                  315
For I can ne'er be conquered but by love,
And you do all for duty. You would free me,
And would be dropped at Athens; was't not so?
OCTAVIA
It was, my Lord.
ANTONY                    Then I must be obliged
To one who loves me not, who to herself                      320
May call me thankless and ungrateful man:
I'll not endure it, no.
VENTIDIUS
I'm glad it pinches there.

307 *scorn* Q1, W2 (scorned Q2, Q3, W1)

OCTAVIA

  Would you triumph o'er poor Octavia's virtue?
  That pride was all I had to bear me up,        325
  That you might think you owed me for your life,
  And owed it to my duty, not my love.
  I have been injured, and my haughty soul
  Could brook but ill the man who slights my bed.

ANTONY

  Therefore you love me not.

OCTAVIA                     Therefore, my Lord,     330
  I should not love you.

ANTONY               Therefore you would leave me?

OCTAVIA

  And therefore I should leave you—if I could.

DOLLABELLA

  Her soul's too great, after such injuries,
  To say she loves; and yet she lets you see it.
  Her modesty and silence plead her cause.       335

ANTONY

  O Dollabella, which way shall I turn?
  I find a secret yielding in my soul;
  But Cleopatra, who would die with me,
  Must she be left? Pity pleads for Octavia,
  But does it not plead more for Cleopatra?     340

VENTIDIUS

  Justice and pity both plead for Octavia;
  For Cleopatra, neither.
  One would be ruined with you, but she first
  Had ruined you; the other you have ruined,
  And yet she would preserve you.         345
  In everything their merits are unequal.

ANTONY

  O my distracted soul!

OCTAVIA               Sweet Heaven compose it!
  Come, come, my Lord, if I can pardon you,
  Methinks you should accept it. Look on these:
  Are they not yours? Or stand they thus neglected   350
  As they are mine? Go to him, children, go;
  Kneel to him, take him by the hand, speak to him,
  For you may speak and he may own you, too,
  Without a blush; and so he cannot all
  His children. Go, I say, and pull him to me,     355

354–5 *all/His children* Antony had three children by Cleopatra.

And pull him to yourselves from that bad woman.
You, Agrippina, hang upon his arms,
And you, Antonia, clasp about his waist:
If he will shake you off, if he will dash you
Against the pavement, you must bear it, children,          360
For you are mine, and I was born to suffer.

               (*Here the* CHILDREN *go to him, etc.*)

VENTIDIUS
  Was ever sight so moving? Emperor!
DOLLABELLA
  Friend!
OCTAVIA  Husband!
BOTH CHILDREN     Father!
ANTONY            I am vanquished: take me,
  Octavia; take me, children; share me all.

                   (*Embracing them*)

  I've been a thriftless debtor to your loves,          365
  And run out much in riot from your stock,
  But all shall be amended.
OCTAVIA         O blest hour!
DOLLABELLA
  O happy change!
VENTIDIUS       My joy stops at my tongue,
  But it has found two channels here for one,
  And bubbles out above.                                  370
ANTONY *to Octavia*
  This is thy triumph. Lead me where thou wilt,
  Even to thy brother's camp.
OCTAVIA         All there are yours.

*Enter* ALEXAS *hastily*

ALEXAS
  The Queen, my mistress, Sir, and yours—
ANTONY              'Tis past.
  Octavia, you shall stay this night: tomorrow
  Caesar and we are one.                                  375

    *Exit, leading* OCTAVIA;   DOLLABELLA *and the* CHILDREN
                  *follow*

---

373–4 *'Tis . . . tomorrow* ed. (printed as one line Q1)

363 *Friend . . . take me* possibly echoing *Coriolanus*, V. iii.

VENTIDIUS
    There's news for you: run, my officious eunuch,
    Be sure to be the first; haste forward;
    Haste, my dear eunuch, haste!         (*Exit*)
ALEXAS
    This downright fighting fool, this thick-skulled hero,
    This blunt, unthinking instrument of death,     380
    With plain dull virtue has outgone my wit.
    Pleasure forsook my earliest infancy;
    The luxury of others robbed my cradle,
    And ravished thence the promise of a man:
    Cast out from Nature, disinherited     385
    Of what her meanest children claim by kind,
    Yet greatness kept me from contempt: that's gone.
    Had Cleopatra followed my advice,
    Then he had been betrayed who now forsakes.
    She dies for love, but she has known its joys:     390
    Gods, is this just that I, who know no joys,
    Must die because she loves?

        *Enter* CLEOPATRA, CHARMION, IRAS, *train*

    Oh Madam, I have seen what blasts my eyes!
    Octavia's here!
CLEOPATRA         Peace with that raven's note.
    I know it too, and now am in     395
    The pangs of death.
ALEXAS         You are no more a queen;
    Egypt is lost.
CLEOPATRA     What tell'st thou me of Egypt?
    My life, my soul is lost! Octavia has him—
    O fatal name to Cleopatra's love!
    My kisses, my embraces now are hers,     400
    While I—but thou hast seen my rival: speak,
    Does she deserve this blessing? Is she fair,
    Bright as a goddess? And is all perfection
    Confined to her? It is. Poor I was made
    Of that coarse matter which, when she was finished,     405
    The gods threw by for rubbish.
ALEXAS
    She's indeed a very miracle.

376 *There's . . . eunuch*, W2 (printed as 2 ll., There's . . . you/My . . .
    eunuch Q1, Q2, Q3, W1)
391 *know* Q3, W1, W2 (knows Q1, Q2)

CLEOPATRA
  Death to my hopes, a miracle!
ALEXAS *bowing*                    A miracle,
  I mean, of goodness; for in beauty, Madam,
  You make all wonders cease.
CLEOPATRA                    I was too rash.                    410
  Take this in part of recompense. But, oh,    (*Giving a ring*)
  I fear thou flatter'st me.
CHARMION
  She comes! She's here!
IRAS                    Fly, Madam, Caesar's sister!
CLEOPATRA
  Were she the sister of the thunderer Jove,
  And bore her brother's lightning in her eyes,                    415
  Thus would I face my rival.

*Meets* OCTAVIA *with* VENTIDIUS, OCTAVIA *bears up to her.*
*Their trains come up on either side*


OCTAVIA
  I need not ask if you are Cleopatra:
  Your haughty carriage—
CLEOPATRA                    Shows I am a queen:
  Nor need I ask you who you are.
OCTAVIA                    A Roman:
  A name that makes, and can unmake, a queen.                    420
CLEOPATRA
  Your lord, the man who serves me, is a Roman.
OCTAVIA
  He was a Roman, till he lost that name
  To be a slave in Egypt; but I come
  To free him thence.
CLEOPATRA                    Peace, peace, my lover's Juno.
  When he grew weary of that household clog,                    425
  He chose my easier bonds.
OCTAVIA                    I wonder not
  Your bonds are easy: you have long been practised
  In that lascivious art. He's not the first
  For whom you spread your snares: let Caesar witness.
CLEOPATRA
  I loved not Caesar: 'twas but gratitude                    430

414 *sister ... Jove* Jupiter's sister and wife, Juno, goddess of marriage,
  avenged herself for his adultery with mortal lovers in many ways; in the
  case of Hercules, this led to the imposition of his labours. See also l. 424.

I paid his love. The worst your malice can
Is but to say the greatest of mankind
Has been my slave. The next, but far above him
In my esteem, is he whom law calls yours,
But whom his love made mine.

OCTAVIA *coming up close to her*          I would view nearer          435
That face which has so long usurped my right,
To find th'inevitable charms that catch
Mankind so sure, that ruined my dear lord.

CLEOPATRA

Oh, you do well to search, for had you known
But half these charms, you had not lost his heart.          440

OCTAVIA

Far be their knowledge from a Roman lady,
Far from a modest wife. Shame of our sex,
Dost thou not blush to own those black endearments
That make sin pleasing?

CLEOPATRA                    You may blush, who want 'em.
If bounteous Nature, if indulgent Heaven          445
Have given me charms to please the bravest man,
Should I not thank 'em? Should I be ashamed,
And not be proud? I am, that he has loved me;
And when I love not him, Heaven change this face
For one like that.

OCTAVIA                    Thou lov'st him not so well.          450

CLEOPATRA

I love him better, and deserve him more.

OCTAVIA

You do not, cannot: you have been his ruin.
Who made him cheap at Rome, but Cleopatra?
Who made him scorned abroad, but Cleopatra?
At Actium who betrayed him? Cleopatra.          455
Who made his children orphans, and poor me
A wretched widow? Only Cleopatra.

CLEOPATRA

Yet she who loves him best is Cleopatra.
If you have suffered, I have suffered more.
You bear the specious title of a wife          460
To gild your cause, and draw the pitying world
To favour it; the world contemns poor me;
For I have lost my honour, lost my fame,
And stained the glory of my royal house,

457 *Cleopatra.* W1, W2 (Cleopatra? Q1, Q2, Q3)

And all to bear the branded name of mistress.                    465
There wants but life, and that too I would lose
For him I love.
OCTAVIA          Be't so, then; take thy wish.

                              *(Exit cum suis)*

CLEOPATRA
And 'tis my wish,
Now he is lost for whom alone I lived.
My sight grows dim, and every object dances                    470
And swims before me in the maze of death.
My spirits, while they were opposed, kept up;
They could not sink beneath a rival's scorn:
But now she's gone, they faint.
ALEXAS                          Mine have had leisure
To recollect their strength, and furnish counsel                    475
To ruin her, who else must ruin you.
CLEOPATRA                          Vain promiser!
Lead me, my Charmion; nay, your hand too, Iras:
My grief has weight enough to sink you both.
Conduct me to some solitary chamber,
And draw the curtains round;                    480
Then leave me to myself, to take alone
My fill of grief:
    There I till death will his unkindness weep,
    As harmless infants moan themselves asleep.

                                          *(Exeunt)*

## Act IV

*Enter* ANTONY, DOLLABELLA

DOLLABELLA
Why would you shift it from yourself on me?
Can you not tell her you must part?
ANTONY                          I cannot.
I could pull out an eye and bid it go,
And t'other should not weep. O Dollabella,
How many deaths are in this word 'Depart'!                    5
I dare not trust my tongue to tell her so:
One look of hers would thaw me into tears,
And I should melt till I were lost again.

s.d. *Enter* Q3, W1 (om. Q1, Q2, W2)

DOLLABELLA
  Then let Ventidius:
  He's rough by nature.
ANTONY                Oh, he'll speak too harshly;     10
  He'll kill her with the news: thou, only thou!
DOLLABELLA
  Nature has cast me in so soft a mould
  That but to hear a story feigned, for pleasure,
  Of some sad lover's death moistens my eyes,
  And robs me of my manhood. I should speak     15
  So faintly, with such fear to grieve her heart,
  She'd not believe it earnest.
ANTONY                Therefore, therefore
  Thou, only thou art fit. Think thyself me,
  And when thou speak'st (but let it first be long),
  Take off the edge from every sharper sound,     20
  And let our parting be as gently made
  As other loves begin: wilt thou do this?
DOLLABELLA
  What you have said so sinks into my soul
  That if I must speak, I shall speak just so.
ANTONY
  I leave you then to your sad task: farewell.     25
  I sent her word to meet you.
                 (*Goes to the door and comes back*)
                 I forgot:
  Let her be told I'll make her peace with mine;
  Her crown and dignity shall be preserved,
  If I have power with Caesar.—Oh, be sure
  To think on that.
DOLLABELLA        Fear not, I will remember.     30
       (ANTONY *goes again to the door and comes back*)
ANTONY
  And tell her too how much I was constrained;
  I did not this but with extremest force.
  Desire her not to hate my memory,
  For I still cherish hers: insist on that.
DOLLABELLA
  Trust me, I'll not forget it.
ANTONY           Then that's all.     35
               (*Goes out and returns again*)
  Wilt thou forgive my fondness this once more?
  Tell her, though we shall never meet again,
  If I should hear she took another love,
  The news would break my heart. Now I must go,

For every time I have returned, I feel                    40
My soul more tender, and my next command
Would be to bid her stay, and ruin both.        (*Exit*)

DOLLABELLA
Men are but children of a larger growth;
Our appetites as apt to change as theirs,
And full as craving too, and full as vain.                45
And yet the soul, shut up in her dark room,
Viewing so clear abroad, at home sees nothing;
But like a mole in earth, busy and blind,
Works all her folly up and casts it outward
To the world's open view: thus I discovered,              50
And blamed, the love of ruined Antony,
Yet wish that I were he, to be so ruined.


*Enter* VENTIDIUS *above*


VENTIDIUS
Alone? And talking to himself? Concerned, too?
Perhaps my guess is right; he loved her once,
And may pursue it still.
DOLLABELLA                    O friendship! Friendship!    55
Ill canst thou answer this; and reason, worse.
Unfaithful in th'attempt, hopeless to win;
And, if I win, undone: mere madness all.
And yet th'occasion's fair. What injury
To him, to wear the robe which he throws by?              60
VENTIDIUS
None, none at all. This happens as I wish,
To ruin her yet more with Antony.


*Enter* CLEOPATRA, *talking with* ALEXAS; CHARMION, IRAS
*on the other side*


DOLLABELLA
She comes! What charms have sorrow on that face!
Sorrow seems pleased to dwell with so much sweetness;
Yet, now and then, a melancholy smile                    65
Breaks loose, like lightning in a winter's night,
And shows a moment's day.
VENTIDIUS
If she should love him too! Her eunuch there!

That porpoise bodes ill weather. Draw, draw nearer,
Sweet devil, that I may hear.
ALEXAS                              Believe me; try                    70

DOLLABELLA *goes over to* CHARMION *and* IRAS; *seems to talk
with them*

To make him jealous: jealousy is like
A polished glass held to the lips when life's in doubt:
If there be breath, 'twill catch the damp, and show it.
CLEOPATRA
I grant you, jealousy's a proof of love,
But 'tis a weak and unavailing medicine:                              75
It puts out the disease, and makes it show,
But has no power to cure.
ALEXAS
'Tis your last remedy, and strongest too.
And then this Dollabella—who so fit
To practise on? He's handsome, valiant, young,                        80
And looks as he were laid for Nature's bait
To catch weak women's eyes.
He stands already more than half suspected
Of loving you: the least kind word or glance
You give this youth will kindle him with love;                        85
Then, like a burning vessel set adrift,
You'll send him down amain before the wind
To fire the heart of jealous Antony.
CLEOPATRA
Can I do this? Ah, no; my love's so true
That I can neither hide it where it is,                                90
Nor show it where it is not. Nature meant me
A wife, a silly, harmless, household dove,
Fond without art, and kind without deceit;
But Fortune, that has made a mistress of me,
Has thrust me out to the wide world, unfurnished                      95
Of falsehood to be happy.
ALEXAS                            Force yourself.
Th'event will be, your lover will return
Doubly desirous to possess the good

69 *That ... nearer*, Q1, Q2, W2 (printed as 2 ll. That ... weather./Draw
... nearer, Q3, W1)
95 *Has* W1, W2 (Hast Q1, Q2, Q3)

69 *porpoise* Porpoises were believed to play before a storm.

Which once he feared to lose.

CLEOPATRA                 I must attempt it;
  But oh, with what regret!             (*Exit* ALEXAS)   100

*She comes up to* DOLLABELLA

VENTIDIUS
  So, now the scene draws near; they're in my reach.

CLEOPATRA *to* DOLLABELLA
  Discoursing with my women! Might not I
  Share in your entertainment?

CHARMION              You have been
  The subject of it, Madam.

CLEOPATRA            How! And how?

IRAS
  Such praises of your beauty!

CLEOPATRA            Mere poetry.         105
  Your Roman wits, your Gallus and Tibullus,
  Have taught you this from Cytheris and Delia.

DOLLABELLA
  Those Roman wits have never been in Egypt;
  Cytheris and Delia else had been unsung:
  I, who have seen—had I been born a poet,     110
  Should choose a nobler name.

CLEOPATRA          You flatter me.
  But 'tis your nation's vice: all of your country
  Are flatterers, and all false. Your friend's like you.
  I'm sure he sent you not to speak these words.

DOLLABELLA
  No, Madam; yet he sent me—

CLEOPATRA         Well, he sent you—     115

DOLLABELLA
  Of a less pleasing errand.

CLEOPATRA         How less pleasing?
  Less to yourself, or me?

DOLLABELLA        Madam, to both;
  For you must mourn, and I must grieve to cause it.

---

106–7 *Gallus ... Delia* Gaius Cornelius Gallus (*c.* 69–26 B.C.), a friend of
  Augustus Caesar, wrote poetry (nearly all lost) dedicated to one of
  Antony's former mistresses, Cytheris, under the pseudonym Lycoris.
  After helping in the defeat of Antony, he fell from favour and com-
  mitted suicide. Tibullus (between 55 and 48 B.C.–A.D. 19) dedicated his
  poetry to Delia and a boy, Marathus.

CLEOPATRA
You, Charmion, and your fellow, stand at distance.—
*Aside* Hold up, my spirits.—Well, now your mournful matter;     120
For I'm prepared, perhaps can guess it too.
DOLLABELLA
I wish you would, for 'tis a thankless office
To tell ill news; and I, of all your sex,
Most fear displeasing you.
CLEOPATRA                            Of all your sex,
I soonest could forgive you, if you should.     125
VENTIDIUS
Most delicate advances! Woman! Woman!
Dear, damned, inconstant sex!
CLEOPATRA                            In the first place,
I am to be forsaken: is't not so?
DOLLABELLA
I wish I could not answer to that question.
CLEOPATRA
Then pass it o'er because it troubles you:     130
I should have been more grieved another time.
Next, I'm to lose my kingdom.—Farewell, Egypt.
Yet is there any more?
DOLLABELLA                    Madam, I fear
Your too deep sense of grief has turned your reason.
CLEOPATRA
No, no, I'm not run mad: I can bear fortune,     135
And love may be expelled by other love,
As poisons are by poisons.
DOLLABELLA
You o'erjoy me, Madam,
To find your griefs so moderately borne.
You've heard the worst; all are not false like him.     140
CLEOPATRA
No; Heaven forbid they should.
DOLLABELLA                            Some men are constant.
CLEOPATRA
And constancy deserves reward, that's certain.
DOLLABELLA
Deserves it not; but give it leave to hope.

132 *Next ... Egypt* cf. *Richard II*, III. ii, 95–6: 'Say, is my kingdom lost?
    Why, 'twas my care;/And what loss is it to be rid of care?' (Klima).
138–9 *You ... borne* cf. *Richard II*, III. ii, 104–5: 'Glad am I that your
    Highness is so armed/To bear the tidings of calamity' (Klima).

VENTIDIUS
I'll swear thou hast my leave. I have enough.
But how to manage this! Well, I'll consider.          (*Exit*)   145
DOLLABELLA
I came prepared
To tell you heavy news, news which, I thought,
Would fright the blood from your pale cheeks to hear:
But you have met it with a cheerfulness
That makes my task more easy; and my tongue,          150
Which on another's message was employed,
Would gladly speak its own.
CLEOPATRA                          Hold, Dollabella.
First tell me, were you chosen by my lord,
Or sought you this employment?
DOLLABELLA
He picked me out, and, as his bosom friend,           155
He charged me with his words.
CLEOPATRA                          The message then
I know was tender, and each accent smooth,
To mollify that rugged word, 'Depart'.
DOLLABELLA
Oh, you mistake: he chose the harshest words;
With fiery eyes and with contracted brows,            160
He coined his face in the severest stamp,
And fury shook his fabric like an earthquake:
He heaved for vent, and burst like bellowing Etna
In sounds scarce human, 'Hence, away forever;
Let her begone, the blot of my renown,                165
And bane of all my hopes:

*All the time of this speech,* CLEOPATRA *seems more and more
concerned, till she sinks quite down.*

Let her be driven as far as men can think
From man's commerce: she'll poison to the centre!'
CLEOPATRA
Oh, I can bear no more!
DOLLABELLA
Help, help! O wretch! O cursed, cursed wretch!        170
What have I done?
CHARMION                Help, chafe her temples, Iras.
IRAS
Bend, bend her forward quickly.
CHARMION                          Heaven be praised,
She comes again.

CLEOPATRA        Oh, let him not approach me.
  Why have you brought me back to this loathed being,
  Th'abode of falsehood, violated vows,                              175
  And injured love? For pity, let me go;
  For if there be a place of long repose,
  I'm sure I want it. My disdainful lord
  Can never break that quiet, nor awake
  The sleeping soul with hollowing in my tomb                        180
  Such words as fright her hence. Unkind, unkind!
DOLLABELLA *kneeling*
  Believe me, 'tis against myself I speak;
  That sure deserves belief. I injured him:
  My friend ne'er spoke those words. Oh, had you seen
  How often he came back, and every time                             185
  With something more obliging and more kind
  To add to what he said: what dear farewells;
  How almost vanquished by his love he parted,
  And leaned to what unwillingly he left.
  I, traitor as I was, for love of you                               190
  (But what can you not do, who made me false?)
  I forged that lie; for whose forgiveness kneels
  This self-accused, self-punished criminal.
CLEOPATRA
  With how much ease believe we what we wish!
  Rise, Dollabella. If you have been guilty,                         195
  I have contributed, and too much love
  Has made me guilty too.
  Th'advance of kindness which I made was feigned,
  To call back fleeting love by jealousy,
  But 'twould not last. Oh, rather let me lose                       200
  Than so ignobly trifle with his heart.
DOLLABELLA
  I find your breast fenced round from human reach,
  Transparent as a rock of solid crystal,
  Seen through, but never pierced. My friend, my friend!
  What endless treasure hast thou thrown away,                       205
  And scattered, like an infant, in the ocean,
  Vain sums of wealth which none can gather thence.
CLEOPATRA
  Could you not beg

---

205-7 *What ... thence* cf. *Othello*, V. ii, 349-51: '... of one whose hand,/
  Like the base Indian, threw a pearl away/Richer than all his tribe'.

An hour's admittance to his private ear?
Like one who wanders through long barren wilds,                210
And yet foreknows no hospitable inn
Is near to succour hunger,
Eats his fill before his painful march:
So would I feed a while my famished eyes
Before we part, for I have far to go,                215
If death be far, and never must return.

*[Enter]* VENTIDIUS *with* OCTAVIA *behind*

VENTIDIUS
  From hence you may discover—
                              [DOLLABELLA *takes* CLEOPATRA's *hand*]
                              Oh, sweet, sweet!
  Would you indeed? The pretty hand in earnest?
DOLLABELLA
  I will, for this reward.—Draw it not back,
  'Tis all I e'er will beg.                220
VENTIDIUS
  They turn upon us.
OCTAVIA                What quick eyes has guilt!
VENTIDIUS
  Seem not to have observed 'em, and go on.

*They enter*

DOLLABELLA
  Saw you the Emperor, Ventidius?
VENTIDIUS                       No.
  I sought him, but I heard that he was private,
  None with him but Hipparchus, his freedman.                225
DOLLABELLA
  Know you his business?
VENTIDIUS                Giving him instructions
  And letters to his brother Caesar.

216 s.d. *Enter* ed. (om. Q1)
217 s.d. DOLLABELLA ... *hand* ed. (*Takes her hand* printed at the end of
    l. 218, Q1, Q2, Q3, W1; at the end of l. 219, W2)
223 DOLLABELLA ... *No* Q3, W1, W2 (printed as 1 line, including speech
    prefix, Q1, Q2)

DOLLABELLA                          Well,
He must be found.    (*Exeunt* DOLLABELLA *and* CLEOPATRA)
OCTAVIA                    Most glorious impudence!
VENTIDIUS
   She looked, methought,
As she would say, 'Take your old man, Octavia;                    230
Thank you, I'm better here'. Well, but what use
Make we of this discovery?
OCTAVIA                          Let it die.
VENTIDIUS
   I pity Dollabella, but she's dangerous:
Her eyes have power beyond Thessalian charms
To draw the moon from heaven; for eloquence,                    235
The sea-green Sirens taught her voice their flattery,
And while she speaks, night steals upon the day,
Unmarked of those that hear; then she's so charming,
Age buds at sight of her, and swells to youth;
The holy priests gaze on her when she smiles,                    240
And with heaved hands, forgetting gravity,
They bless her wanton eyes; even I, who hate her,
With a malignant joy behold such beauty,
And while I curse, desire it. Antony
Must needs have some remains of passion still,                    245
Which may ferment into a worse relapse
If now not fully cured. I know this minute
With Caesar he's endeavouring her peace.
OCTAVIA
   You have prevailed.—But for a farther purpose
                          (*Walks off*)

---

231 *Thank ... use* ed. (printed as 2 ll. Thank ... here./Well ... use Q1)

234 *Thessalian* '... Thessalian witches, whom no boldness of imaginary
    horror can outdo ... By their spells love steals into insensible hearts
    against the decree of destiny, and austere old age burns with forbidden
    passion' (Lucan, *The Civil War* [*Pharsalia*], with a translation by J. D.
    Duff, London: Loeb Classical Library, 1928, pp. 337–9).
236 *Sirens*
        Unblest the man whom music wins to stay
        Nigh the curst shore, and listen to the lay;
        No more that wretch shall view the joys of life,
        His blooming offspring, or his beauteous wife.
                    (*Odyssey XII*, Pope's translation, ll. 53–6)
240–2 *The holy ... eyes* cf. Shakespeare, *Antony and Cleopatra*, II. ii,
    243–4: '... the holy priests/Bless her when she is riggish'.

I'll prove how he will relish this discovery.                    250
What, make a strumpet's peace! It swells my heart;
It must not, sha' not be.
VENTIDIUS                    His guards appear.
Let me begin, and you shall second me.

*Enter* ANTONY [*and* GUARDS]

ANTONY
Octavia, I was looking you, my love.
What, are your letters ready? I have given                    255
My last instructions.
OCTAVIA                    Mine, my Lord, are written.
ANTONY
Ventidius!                                        (*Drawing him aside*)
VENTIDIUS    My Lord?
ANTONY                    A word in private.
When saw you Dollabella?
VENTIDIUS                    Now, my Lord,
He parted hence, and Cleopatra with him.
ANTONY
Speak softly. 'Twas by my command he went,                    260
To bear my last farewell.
VENTIDIUS *aloud*                    It looked indeed
Like your farewell.
ANTONY                    More softly.—My farewell?
What secret meaning have you in those words
Of 'my farewell'? He did it by my order.
VENTIDIUS *aloud*
Then he obeyed your order. I suppose                    265
You bid him do it with all gentleness,
All kindness, and all—love.
ANTONY                    How she mourned,
The poor forsaken creature!
VENTIDIUS
She took it as she ought; she bore your parting
As she did Caesar's, as she would another's,                    270
Were a new love to come.
ANTONY *aloud*                    Thou dost belie her,
Most basely and maliciously belie her.
VENTIDIUS
I thought not to displease you; I have done.

253 s.d. *and* GUARDS ed. (om. Q1)

OCTAVIA *coming up*
  You seem disturbed, my Lord.
ANTONY                              A very trifle.
  Retire, my love.
VENTIDIUS          It was indeed a trifle.                    275
  He sent—
ANTONY *angrily* No more. Look how thou disobey'st me;
  Thy life shall answer it.
OCTAVIA                      Then 'tis no trifle.
VENTIDIUS *to* OCTAVIA
  'Tis less, a very nothing: you too saw it,
  As well as I, and therefore 'tis no secret.
ANTONY
  She saw it!
VENTIDIUS          Yes. She saw young Dollabella—          280
ANTONY
  Young Dollabella!
VENTIDIUS                      Young; I think him young,
  And handsome too, and so do others think him.
  But what of that? He went by your command,
  Indeed 'tis probable, with some kind message,
  For she received it graciously: she smiled,          285
  And then he grew familiar with her hand,
  Squeezed it, and worried it with ravenous kisses.
  She blushed, and sighed, and smiled, and blushed again;
  At last she took occasion to talk softly,
  And brought her cheek up close, and leaned on his,          290
  At which he whispered kisses back on hers,
  And then she cried aloud that 'constancy
  Should be rewarded'.
OCTAVIA                      This I saw and heard.
ANTONY
  What woman was it, whom you heard and saw
  So playful with my friend? Not Cleopatra?          295
VENTIDIUS
  Even she, my Lord.
ANTONY                      My Cleopatra?

---

295 *So . . . Cleopatra?* ed. (printed as 2 ll., So . . . friend?/Not Cleopatra? Q1)

---

288 *She . . . again* cf. Daniel, *Cleopatra*, 1287–9: '[She] reads, and smiles,
    and stays, and doth begin/Again to read, then blushed, and then was
    pale,/And having ended with a sigh . . .'

VENTIDIUS
Your Cleopatra;
Dollabella's Cleopatra;
Every man's Cleopatra.
ANTONY
Thou liest.
VENTIDIUS    I do not lie, my Lord. 300
Is this so strange? Should mistresses be left,
And not provide against a time of change?
You know she's not much used to lonely nights.
ANTONY
I'll think no more on't.
I know 'tis false, and see the plot betwixt you. 305
You needed not have gone this way, Octavia.
What harms it you that Cleopatra's just?
She's mine no more. I see, and I forgive:
Urge it no farther, love.
OCTAVIA                Are you concerned
That she's found false?
ANTONY             I should be, were it so; 310
For though 'tis past, I would not that the world
Should tax my former choice, that I loved one
Of so light note. But I forgive you both.
VENTIDIUS
What has my age deserved, that you should think
I would abuse your ears with perjury? 315
If Heaven be true, she's false.
ANTONY             Though Heaven and earth
Should witness it, I'll not believe her tainted.
VENTIDIUS
I'll bring you then a witness
From Hell to prove her so.
    *Seeing* ALEXAS *just entering, and starting back*
                Nay, go not back;
For stay you must, and shall.
ALEXAS           What means my Lord? 320
VENTIDIUS
To make you do what most you hate: speak truth.
You are of Cleopatra's private counsel,

319 *not* Q1, Q2, W2 (om. Q3, W1)

---

297-9 *Your ... Cleopatra* cf. *Much Ado About Nothing*, III. ii, 94-5:
'Leonato's Hero, your Hero, every man's Hero'.

Of her bed-counsel, her lascivious hours;
Are conscious of each nightly change she makes,
And watch her, as Chaldeans do the moon;            325
Can tell what signs she passes through, what day.

ALEXAS
My noble Lord—

VENTIDIUS            My most illustrious pander,
No fine set speech, no cadence, no turned periods,
But a plain homespun truth is what I ask.
I did myself o'erhear your Queen make love            330
To Dollabella. Speak, for I will know,
By your confession, what more passed betwixt 'em,
How near the business draws to your employment,
And when the happy hour.

ANTONY
Speak truth, Alexas: whether it offend            335
Or please Ventidius, care not: justify
Thy injured Queen from malice; dare his worst.

OCTAVIA aside
See how he gives him courage! How he fears
To find her false, and shuts his eyes to truth,
Willing to be misled!            340

ALEXAS
As far as love may plead for woman's frailty,
Urged by desert and greatness of the lover,
So far, divine Octavia, may my Queen
Stand even excused to you for loving him
Who is your lord; so far from brave Ventidius            345
May her past actions hope a fair report.

ANTONY
'Tis well and truly spoken: mark, Ventidius.

ALEXAS
To you, most noble Emperor, her strong passion
Stands not excused, but wholly justified.
Her beauty's charms alone, without her crown,            350
From Ind and Meroe drew the distant vows
Of sighing kings, and at her feet were laid
The sceptres of the earth, exposed on heaps,
To choose where she would reign:

---

325 *Chaldeans* Assyrian astronomers and astrologers (Lucretius, *De Rerum Natura*, V, 726).
351 *Ind* India or the East in general. *Meroe* a region of the upper Nile.

She thought a Roman only could deserve her,                    355
And of all Romans, only Antony;
And, to be less than wife to you, disdained
Their lawful passion.
ANTONY                          'Tis but truth.
ALEXAS
And yet, though love and your unmatched desert
Have drawn her from the due regard of honour,                 360
At last Heaven opened her unwilling eyes
To see the wrongs she offered fair Octavia,
Whose holy bed she lawlessly usurped:
The sad effects of this improsperous war
Confirmed those pious thoughts.
VENTIDIUS *aside*                       Oh, wheel you there?    365
Observe him now; the man begins to mend,
And talk substantial reason.—Fear not, eunuch;
The Emperor has given thee leave to speak.
ALEXAS
Else had I never dared t'offend his ears
With what the last necessity has urged                        370
On my forsaken mistress; yet I must not
Presume to say her heart is wholly altered.
ANTONY
No, dare not for thy life, I charge thee dare not
Pronounce that fatal word!
OCTAVIA *aside*
Must I bear this? Good Heaven afford me patience.             375
VENTIDIUS
On, sweet eunuch; my dear half-man, proceed.
ALEXAS
Yet Dollabella
Has loved her long. He, next my godlike lord,
Deserves her best; and should she meet his passion,
Rejected as she is by him she loved—                          380
ANTONY
Hence from my sight, for I can bear no more!
Let Furies drag thee quick to Hell; let all
The longer damned have rest; each torturing hand
Do thou employ, till Cleopatra comes;

363 *lawlessly* Q1, W2 (lawfully Q2, Q3, W1)
382–3 *let all ... rest* Q1, W2 (om. Q2, Q3, W1)

Then join thou too, and help to torture her!                385
   (*Exit* ALEXAS, *thrust out by* ANTONY)

OCTAVIA
'Tis not well;
Indeed, my Lord, 'tis much unkind to me,
To show this passion, this extreme concernment
For an abandoned, faithless prostitute.

ANTONY
Octavia, leave me. I am much disordered.                390
Leave me, I say.

OCTAVIA    My Lord?

ANTONY      I bid you leave me.

VENTIDIUS
Obey him, Madam: best withdraw a while,
And see how this will work.

OCTAVIA
Wherein have I offended you, my Lord,
That I am bid to leave you? Am I false                395
Or infamous? Am I a Cleopatra?
Were I she,
Base as she is, you would not bid me leave you,
But hang upon my neck, take slight excuses,
And fawn upon my falsehood.

ANTONY     'Tis too much,                400
Too much, Octavia: I am pressed with sorrows
Too heavy to be borne, and you add more.
I would retire, and recollect what's left
Of man within, to aid me.

OCTAVIA    You would mourn
In private for your love, who has betrayed you.                405
You did but half return to me: your kindness
Lingered behind with her. I hear, my Lord,
You make conditions for her,
And would include her treaty. Wondrous proofs
Of love to me!

ANTONY   Are you my friend, Ventidius?                410
Or are you turned a Dollabella too,
And let this Fury loose?

VENTIDIUS    Oh, be advised,
Sweet Madam, and retire.

OCTAVIA
Yes, I will go, but never to return.
You shall no more be haunted with this Fury.                415
My Lord, my Lord, love will not always last
When urged with long unkindness and disdain.

Take her again whom you prefer to me:
She stays but to be called. Poor cozened man!
Let a feigned parting give her back your heart, 420
Which a feigned love first got. For injured me,
Though my just sense of wrongs forbid my stay,
My duty shall be yours.
To the dear pledges of our former love
My tenderness and care shall be transferred, 425
And they shall cheer, by turns, my widowed nights.
So, take my last farewell, for I despair
To have you whole, and scorn to take you half.　　(*Exit*)

VENTIDIUS

I combat Heaven, which blasts my best designs:
My last attempt must be to win her back, 430
But, oh, I fear, in vain.　　(*Exit*)

ANTONY

Why was I framed with this plain, honest heart,
Which knows not to disguise its griefs and weakness,
But bears its workings outward to the world?
I should have kept the mighty anguish in, 435
And forced a smile at Cleopatra's falsehood:
Octavia had believed it, and had stayed;
But I am made a shallow-forded stream,
Seen to the bottom, all my clearness scorned,
And all my faults exposed.—See where he comes 440

*Enter* DOLLABELLA

Who has profaned the sacred name of friend,
And worn it into vileness!
With how secure a brow, and specious form,
He gilds the secret villain! Sure that face
Was meant for honesty, but Heaven mismatched it, 445
And furnished treason out with Nature's pomp
To make its work more easy.

DOLLABELLA　　　　　　O my friend!

ANTONY

Well, Dollabella, you performed my message?

DOLLABELLA

I did, unwillingly.

ANTONY　　　　　Unwillingly?
Was it so hard for you to bear our parting? 450
You should have wished it.

DOLLABELLA　　　　　　Why?

ANTONY                              Because you love me.
  And she received my message with as true,
  With as unfeigned a sorrow as you brought it?
DOLLABELLA
  She loves you, even to madness.
ANTONY                              Oh, I know it.
  You, Dollabella, do not better know                         455
  How much she loves me. And should I
  Forsake this beauty, this all-perfect creature?
DOLLABELLA
  I could not, were she mine.
ANTONY                              And yet you first
  Persuaded me: how come you altered since?
DOLLABELLA
  I said at first I was not fit to go:                         460
  I could not hear her sighs, and see her tears,
  But pity must prevail. And so perhaps
  It may again with you, for I have promised
  That she should take her last farewell; and see,
  She comes to claim my word.

*Enter* CLEOPATRA

ANTONY                              False Dollabella!                  465
DOLLABELLA
  What's false, my Lord?
ANTONY                              Why, Dollabella's false,
  And Cleopatra's false; both false and faithless.
  Draw near, you well-joined wickedness, you serpents,
  Whom I have in my kindly bosom warmed
  Till I am stung to death.
DOLLABELLA                          My Lord, have I                   470
  Deserved to be thus used?
CLEOPATRA                          Can Heaven prepare
  A newer torment? Can it find a curse
  Beyond our separation?
ANTONY                              Yes, if fate
  Be just, much greater: Heaven should be ingenious
  In punishing such crimes. The rolling stone                   475

475–6 *rolling stone . . . gnawing vulture* In Tartarus, Sisyphus was set to roll a
    stone up a hill as punishment for rape and the pursuit of tyrannical
    power, and Tityus' heart was devoured by a vulture for having at-
    tempted to rape Diana, goddess of chastity, at Juno's instigation.

And gnawing vulture were slight pains, invented
When Jove was young, and no examples known
Of mighty ills; but you have ripened sin
To such a monstrous growth, 'twill pose the gods
To find an equal torture. Two, two such—                480
Oh, there's no farther name! Two such—to me,
To me who locked my soul within your breasts,
Had no desires, no joys, no life, but you:
When half the globe was mine, I gave it you
In dowry with my heart; I had no use,                   485
No fruit of all, but you; a friend and mistress
Was what the world could give. O Cleopatra!
O Dollabella! How could you betray
This tender heart, which with an infant fondness
Lay lulled betwixt your bosoms, and there slept         490
Secure of injured faith?

DOLLABELLA                    If she has wronged you,
Heaven, Hell, and you revenge it.

ANTONY                                 If she wronged me!
Thou wouldst evade thy part of guilt; but swear
Thou lov'st not her.

DOLLABELLA           Not so as I love you.

ANTONY
Not so? Swear, swear, I say, thou dost not love her.     495

DOLLABELLA
No more than friendship will allow.

ANTONY                              No more?
Friendship allows thee nothing: thou art perjured.—
And yet thou didst not swear thou lov'dst her not,
But not so much, no more. O trifling hypocrite,
Who dar'st not own to her thou dost not love,            500
Nor own to me thou dost! Ventidius heard it;
Octavia saw it.

CLEOPATRA        They are enemies.

ANTONY
Alexas is not so. He, he confessed it;
He who, next Hell, best knew it, he avowed it.
(*To* DOLLABELLA) Why do I seek a proof beyond yourself?  505
You, whom I sent to bear my last farewell,
Returned to plead her stay.

DOLLABELLA                 What shall I answer?
If to have loved be guilt, then I have sinned;
But if to have repented of that love
Can wash away my crime, I have repented.                 510
Yet, if I have offended past forgiveness,

Let not her suffer: she is innocent.

CLEOPATRA
Ah, what will not a woman do who'loves!
What means will she refuse to keep that heart
Where all her joys are placed! 'Twas I encouraged,          515
'Twas I blew up the fire that scorched his soul,
To make you jealous, and by that regain you.
But all in vain: I could not counterfeit;
In spite of all the dams, my love broke o'er,
And drowned my heart again. Fate took th'occasion,         520
And thus one minute's feigning has destroyed
My whole life's truth.

ANTONY                Thin cobweb arts of falsehood,
Seen and broke through at first.

DOLLABELLA                        Forgive your mistress.

CLEOPATRA
Forgive your friend.

ANTONY                You have convinced yourselves;
You plead each other's cause: what witness have you          525
That you but meant to raise my jealousy?

CLEOPATRA
Ourselves, and Heaven.

ANTONY
Guilt witnesses for guilt. Hence, love and friendship.
You have no longer place in human breasts;
These two have driven you out. Avoid my sight:              530
I would not kill the man whom I have loved,
And cannot hurt the woman; but avoid me:
I do not know how long I can be tame,
For if I stay one minute more to think
How I am wronged, my justice and revenge                    535
Will cry so loud within me that my pity
Will not be heard for either.

DOLLABELLA                        Heaven has but
Our sorrow for our sins, and then delights
To pardon erring man: sweet mercy seems
Its darling attribute, which limits justice,                540
As if there were degrees in infinite,
And infinite would rather want perfection
Than punish to extent.

ANTONY                    I can forgive
A foe, but not a mistress and a friend.
Treason is there in its most horrid shape                    545

531 *have* W2 (om. Q1, Q2, Q3, W1)

Where trust is greatest, and the soul resigned
Is stabbed by its own guards. I'll hear no more;
Hence from my sight forever.

CLEOPATRA                How? Forever!
I cannot go one moment from your sight,
And must I go forever?                       550
My joys, my only joys, are centred here:
What place have I to go to? My own kingdom?
That I have lost for you; or to the Romans?
They hate me for your sake; or must I wander
The wide world o'er, a helpless, banished woman,     555
Banished for love of you, banished from you?
Aye, there's the banishment! Oh, hear me, hear me
With strictest justice, for I beg no favour,
And if I have offended you, then kill me,
But do not banish me.

ANTONY              I must not hear you.       560
I have a fool within me takes your part,
But honour stops my ears.

CLEOPATRA              For pity hear me!
Would you cast off a slave who followed you,
Who crouched beneath your spurn?—He has no pity!
See if he gives one tear to my departure,         565
One look, one kind farewell: oh, iron heart!
Let all the gods look down, and judge betwixt us,
If he did ever love!

ANTONY
                 No more: Alexas!

DOLLABELLA
A perjured villain!

ANTONY *to* CLEOPATRA Your Alexas, yours.

CLEOPATRA
Oh, 'twas his plot, his ruinous design,           570
T'engage you in my love by jealousy.
Hear him; confront him with me; let him speak.

ANTONY
I have, I have.

CLEOPATRA      And if he clear me not—

ANTONY
Your creature! One who hangs upon your smiles,
Watches your eye to say or to unsay           575
Whate'er you please! I am not to be moved.

CLEOPATRA
Then must we part? Farewell, my cruel Lord!
Th'appearance is against me, and I go,

Unjustified, forever from your sight.
How I have loved, you know; how yet I love,                    580
My only comfort is, I know myself.
I love you more, even now you are unkind,
Than when you loved me most; so well, so truly,
I'll never strive against it, but die pleased
To think you once were mine.                                   585

ANTONY
Good Heaven, they weep at parting!
Must I weep too? That calls 'em innocent.
I must not weep; and yet I must, to think
That I must not forgive.—
Live, but live wretched; 'tis but just you should,            590
Who made me so: live from each other's sight;
Let me not hear you meet; set all the earth
And all the seas betwixt your sundered loves;
View nothing common but the sun and skies.
Now all take several ways,                                     595
  And each your own sad fate, with mine, deplore:
  That you were false, and I could trust no more.
                                        (*Exeunt severally*)


## Act V

*Enter* CLEOPATRA, CHARMION, IRAS

CHARMION
Be juster, Heaven; such virtue punished thus
Will make us think that chance rules all above,
And shuffles with a random hand the lots
Which man is forced to draw.

CLEOPATRA
I could tear out these eyes, that gained his heart            5
And had not power to keep it. Oh the curse
Of doting on, even when I find it dotage!
Bear witness, gods, you heard him bid me go;
You, whom he mocked with imprecating vows
Of promised faith.—I'll die, I will not bear it!             10
                (*She pulls out her dagger, and they hold her*)
You may hold me—
But I can keep my breath; I can die inward,
And choke this love.

s.d. *enter* Q3, W1 (om. Q1, Q2, W2)

*Enter* ALEXAS

IRAS                  Help, O Alexas, help!
  The Queen grows desperate; her soul struggles in her
  With all the agonies of love and rage,             15
  And strives to force its passage.
CLEOPATRA               Let me go.
  Art thou there, traitor!—Oh,
  Oh, for a little breath, to vent my rage!
  Give, give me way, and let me loose upon him.
ALEXAS
  Yes, I deserve it, for my ill-timed truth.        20
  Was it for me to prop
  The ruins of a falling majesty?
  To place myself beneath the mighty flaw,
  Thus to be crushed and pounded into atoms
  By its o'erwhelming weight? 'Tis too presuming    25
  For subjects to preserve that wilful power
  Which courts its own destruction.
CLEOPATRA                  I would reason
  More calmly with you. Did not you o'errule
  And force my plain, direct, and open love
  Into these crooked paths of jealousy?         30
  Now, what's th'event? Octavia is removed,
  But Cleopatra's banished. Thou, thou villain,
  Hast pushed my boat to open sea, to prove,
  At my sad cost, if thou canst steer it back.
  It cannot be; I'm lost too far; I'm ruined.     35
  Hence, thou impostor, traitor, monster, devil!—
  I can no more: thou, and my griefs, have sunk
  Me down so low that I want voice to curse thee.
ALEXAS
  Suppose some shipwrecked seaman near the shore,
  Dropping and faint with climbing up the cliff;    40
  If, from above, some charitable hand
  Pull him to safety, hazarding himself
  To draw the other's weight, would he look back
  And curse him for his pains? The case is yours:
  But one step more, and you have gained the height.   45
CLEOPATRA
  Sunk, never more to rise.

33 *Hast* W2 (Has Q1, Q2, Q3, W1)

ALEXAS
  Octavia's gone, and Dollabella banished.
  Believe me, Madam, Antony is yours.
  His heart was never lost, but started off
  To jealousy, love's last retreat and covert,                    50
  Where it lies hid in shades, watchful in silence,
  And listening for the sound that calls it back.
  Some other, any man ('tis so advanced),
  May perfect this unfinished work, which I
  (Unhappy only to myself) have left                    55
  So easy to his hand.
CLEOPATRA           Look well thou do't; else—
ALEXAS
  Else what your silence threatens.—Antony
  Is mounted up the Pharos, from whose turret
  He stands surveying our Egyptian galleys
  Engaged with Caesar's fleet: now death or conquest.                    60
  If the first happen, fate acquits my promise;
  If we o'ercome, the conqueror is yours.
                       (*A distant shout within*)

CHARMION
  Have comfort, Madam: did you mark that shout?
                       (*Second shout nearer*)

IRAS
  Hark! They redouble it.
ALEXAS               'Tis from the port.
  The loudness shows it near: good news, kind Heavens!                    65
CLEOPATRA
  Osiris make it so!


*Enter* SERAPION

SERAPION         Where, where's the Queen?
ALEXAS
  How frightfully the holy coward stares,
  As if not yet recovered of th'assault,
  When all his gods, and, what's more dear to him,
  His offerings, were at stake!
SERAPION           O horror, horror!                    70
  Egypt has been; our latest hour is come;
  The queen of nations from her ancient seat

66 *Osiris* god of death, the husband of Isis, goddess of fertility. See I, 1,
s.d.

Is sunk forever in the dark abyss;
Time has unrolled her glories to the last,
And now closed up the volume.

CLEOPATRA                    Be more plain.                    75
Say whence thou com'st—though fate is in thy face,
Which from thy haggard eyes looks wildly out,
And threatens ere thou speak'st.

SERAPION                I came from Pharos;
From viewing (spare me, and imagine it)
Our land's last hope, your navy—

CLEOPATRA                    Vanquished?
SERAPION                            No.                    80
They fought not.

CLEOPATRA            Then they fled.
SERAPION                        Nor that. I saw,
With Antony, your well-appointed fleet
Row out; and thrice he waved his hand on high,
And thrice with cheerful cries they shouted back:
'Twas then false Fortune, like a fawning strumpet            85
About to leave the bankrupt prodigal,
With a dissembled smile would kiss at parting
And flatter to the last. The well-timed oars
Now dipped from every bank, now smoothly run
To meet the foe; and soon indeed they met,                    90
But not as foes. In few, we saw their caps
On either side thrown up; th'Egyptian galleys,
Received like friends, passed through and fell behind
The Roman rear; and now they all come forward,
And ride within the port.

CLEOPATRA                    Enough, Serapion:                    95
I've heard my doom. This needed not, you gods.
When I lost Antony, your work was done;
'Tis but superfluous malice. Where's my Lord?
How bears he this last blow?

76 *com'st* Q1 corrected, Q2, Q3, W1 (cam'st Q1 uncorrected, W2)
79 *spare* Q1 corrected, Q2, Q3, W1, W2 (share Q1 uncorrected)
87 *dissembled* Q1, W2 (dissembling Q2, Q3, W1)

90–3 *soon . . . friends* cf. Shakespeare, *Antony and Cleopatra*, IV. xii, 9–13:
All is lost!
This foul Egyptian hath betrayed me.
My fleet hath yielded to the foe, and yonder
They cast their caps up and carouse together
Like friends long lost.

SERAPION

His fury cannot be expressed by words. 100
Thrice he attempted headlong to have fallen
Full on his foes, and aimed at Caesar's galley;
Withheld, he raves on you, cries he's betrayed.
Should he now find you—

ALEXAS                                        Shun him; seek your safety
Till you can clear your innocence.

CLEOPATRA                            I'll stay. 105

ALEXAS

You must not: haste you to your monument,
While I make speed to Caesar.

CLEOPATRA                            Caesar! No,
I have no business with him.

ALEXAS                            I can work him
To spare your life, and let this madman perish.

CLEOPATRA

Base, fawning wretch! Wouldst thou betray him too? 110
Hence from my sight: I will not hear a traitor;
'Twas thy design brought all this ruin on us.
Serapion, thou art honest: counsel me;
But haste, each moment's precious.

SERAPION

Retire; you must not yet see Antony. 115
He who began this mischief,
'Tis just he tempt the danger: let him clear you;
And since he offered you his servile tongue
To gain a poor precarious life from Caesar,
Let him expose that fawning eloquence, 120
And speak to Antony.

ALEXAS                      O Heavens! I dare not;
I meet my certain death.

CLEOPATRA                      Slave, thou deserv'st it.
Not that I fear my Lord will I avoid him.
I know him noble: when he banished me
And thought me false, he scorned to take my life; 125
But I'll be justified, and then die with him.

ALEXAS

Oh pity me, and let me follow you!

CLEOPATRA

To death, if thou stir hence. Speak, if thou canst,
Now for thy life, which basely thou wouldst save,

102 *at* Q1, Q2, W2 (om. Q3, W1)

While mine I prize at this. Come, good Serapion. 130
(*Exeunt* CLEOPATRA, SERAPION, CHARMION, IRAS)

ALEXAS
Oh that I less could fear to lose this being,
Which, like a snowball in my coward hand,
The more 'tis grasped, the faster melts away.
Poor reason! What a wretched aid art thou!
For still, in spite of thee, 135
These two long lovers, soul and body, dread
Their final separation. Let me think:
What can I say to save myself from death?
No matter what becomes of Cleopatra.

ANTONY *within*
Which way? Where?
VENTIDIUS *within* This leads to the monument. 140

ALEXAS
Ah me! I hear him, yet I'm unprepared.
My gift of lying's gone,
And this court-devil, which I so oft have raised,
Forsakes me at my need. I dare not stay,
Yet cannot far go hence. (*Exit*) 145

*Enter* ANTONY *and* VENTIDIUS

ANTONY
O happy Caesar! Thou hast men to lead:
Think not 'tis thou hast conquered Antony,
But Rome has conquered Egypt. I'm betrayed.

VENTIDIUS
Curse on this treacherous train!
Their soil and Heaven infect 'em all with baseness, 150
And their young souls come tainted to the world
With the first breath they draw.

ANTONY
Th'original villain sure no god created;
He was a bastard of the sun by Nile,
Aped into man, with all his mother's mud 155
Crusted about his soul.
VENTIDIUS The nation is
One universal traitor, and their Queen
The very spirit and extract of 'em all.

ANTONY
Is there yet left
A possibility of aid from valour? 160
Is there one god unsworn to my destruction?

The least unmortgaged hope? For if there be,
Methinks I cannot fall beneath the fate
Of such a boy as Caesar.
The world's one half is yet in Antony,                    165
And from each limb of it that's hewed away
The soul comes back to me.
VENTIDIUS                              There yet remain
Three legions in the town: the last assault
Lopped off the rest. If death be your design,
As I must wish it now, these are sufficient               170
To make a heap about us of dead foes,
An honest pile for burial.
ANTONY                              They're enough.
We'll not divide our stars, but side by side
Fight emulous, and with malicious eyes
Survey each other's acts; so every death                  175
Thou giv'st, I'll take on me as a just debt,
And pay thee back a soul.
VENTIDIUS
Now you shall see I love you. Not a word
Of chiding more. By my few hours of life,
I am so pleased with this brave Roman fate                180
That I would not be Caesar, to outlive you.
When we put off this flesh and mount together,
I shall be shown to all th'ethereal crowd:
'Lo, this is he who died with Antony!'
ANTONY
Who knows but we may pierce through all their troops,     185
And reach my veterans yet? 'Tis worth the tempting
T'o'erleap this gulf of fate,
And leave our wondering destinies behind.

*Enter* ALEXAS, *trembling*

VENTIDIUS
See, see that villain!
See Cleopatra stamped upon that face,                     190
With all her cunning, all her arts of falsehood!

177 *back* Q1 corrected, Q2, Q3, W1 (in Q1 uncorrected, W2)
188 *wondering* Q1, W2 (wandering Q2, Q3, W1)

165–7 *The world's . . . to me* See H. Kossmann, 'A note on Dryden's *All
For Love*, V. 165 ff.', *English Studies*, 31 (1950), 99–100.

How she looks out through those dissembling eyes!
How he has set his countenance for deceit,
And promises a lie before he speaks!
Let me dispatch him first.                    (*Drawing*)
ALEXAS                   Oh spare me, spare me!          195
ANTONY
Hold, he's not worth your killing. On thy life,
Which thou mayst keep because I scorn to take it,
No syllable to justify thy Queen;
Save thy base tongue its office.
ALEXAS                        Sir, she's gone
Where she shall never be molested more          200
By love, or you.
ANTONY            Fled to her Dollabella!
Die, traitor! I revoke my promise! Die!
                                 (*Going to kill him*)
ALEXAS
Oh hold: she is not fled.
ANTONY                    She is; my eyes
Are open to her falsehood. My whole life
Has been a golden dream of love and friendship.     205
But now I wake, I'm like a merchant roused
From soft repose to see his vessel sinking,
And all his wealth cast o'er. Ingrateful woman!
Who followed me but as the swallow summer,
Hatching her young ones in my kindly beams,       210
Singing her flatteries to my morning wake;
But now my winter comes, she spreads her wings,
And seeks the spring of Caesar.
ALEXAS                        Think not so:
Her fortunes have in all things mixed with yours.
Had she betrayed her naval force to Rome,         215
How easily might she have gone to Caesar,
Secure by such a bribe!
VENTIDIUS               She sent it first,
To be more welcome after.
ANTONY                    'Tis too plain;
Else would she have appeared to clear herself.

193 *has set* Q1, W2 (sets Q2, Q3, W1)

---

208–13 *Ingrateful . . . Caesar* cf. Daniel, *Cleopatra*, 43–5: 'Witness these
gallant fortune-following trains,/These summer swallows of felicity/
Gone with the heat . . .'

ALEXAS
   Too fatally she has: she could not bear                    220
   To be accused by you, but shut herself
   Within her monument, looked down and sighed,
   While from her unchanged face the silent tears
   Dropped, as they had not leave, but stole their parting;
   Some undistinguished words she inly murmured;                    225
   At last she raised her eyes, and with such looks
   As dying Lucrece cast—
ANTONY                    My heart forebodes—
VENTIDIUS
   All for the best; go on.
ALEXAS                    She snatched her poniard,
   And, ere we could prevent the fatal blow,
   Plunged it within her breast, then turned to me:                    230
   'Go, bear my lord', said she, 'my last farewell,
   And ask him if he yet suspect my faith'.
   More she was saying, but death rushed betwixt.
   She half pronounced your name with her last breath,
   And buried half within her.
VENTIDIUS                    Heaven be praised.                    235
ANTONY
   Then art thou innocent, my poor dear love?
   And art thou dead?
   Oh those two words! Their sound should be divided:
   Hadst thou been false, and died; or hadst thou lived,
   And hadst been true—but innocence and death!                    240
   This shows not well above. Then what am I,
   The murderer of this truth, this innocence?
   Thoughts cannot form themselves in words so horrid
   As can express my guilt!
VENTIDIUS
   Is't come to this? The gods have been too gracious,                    245
   And thus you thank 'em for't.
ANTONY *to* ALEXAS                    Why stay'st thou here?
   Is it for thee to spy upon my soul,
   And see its inward mourning? Get thee hence!

227 *Lucrece* The rape of Lucrece by Sextus Tarquinius, son of the Roman
   King Lucius Tarquinius Superbus, and her subsequent suicide led the
   Roman people under Lucius Junius Brutus to exile the Tarquins and
   establish the Roman Republic, which itself was superseded when
   Octavius became the Emperor Augustus after the events described in
   *All For Love.*

Thou are not worthy to behold what now
Becomes a Roman emperor to perform.                    250
ALEXAS *aside*
He loves her still:
His grief betrays it. Good! The joy to find
She's yet alive completes the reconcilement.
I've saved myself and her. But, oh! The Romans!
Fate comes too fast upon my wit,                    255
Hunts me too hard, and meets me at each double.    (*Exit*)
VENTIDIUS
Would she had died a little sooner, though,
Before Octavia went: you might have treated.
Now 'twill look tame, and would not be received.
Come, rouse yourself, and let's die warm together.                    260
ANTONY
I will not fight: there's no more work for war.
The business of my angry hours is done.
VENTIDIUS
Caesar is at your gates.
ANTONY                     Why, let him enter;
He's welcome now.
VENTIDIUS
What lethargy has crept into your soul?                    265
ANTONY
'Tis but a scorn of life, and just desire
To free myself from bondage.
VENTIDIUS                          Do it bravely.
ANTONY
I will; but not by fighting. O Ventidius!
What should I fight for now? My Queen is dead.
I was but great for her; my power, my empire                    270
Were but my merchandise to buy her love,
And conquered kings, my factors. Now she's dead,
Let Caesar take the world—
An empty circle, since the jewel's gone
Which made it worth my strife; my being's nauseous,                    275
For all the bribes of life are gone away.

265 *What . . . soul* cf. Sedley, *Antony and Cleopatra*, I. ii, 227: 'You should
   my lethargy of honour chide'.
273–5 *Let . . . strife* cf. Shakespeare, *Antony and Cleopatra*, IV. xv, 75–8:
                     It were for me
            To throw my sceptre at the injurious gods;
            To tell them that this world did equal theirs
            Till they had stolen our jewel.

VENTIDIUS
  Would you be taken?
ANTONY              Yes, I would be taken,
  But as a Roman ought—dead, my Ventidius;
  For I'll convey my soul from Caesar's reach,
  And lay down life myself. 'Tis time the world       280
  Should have a lord, and know whom to obey.
  We two have kept its homage in suspense,
  And bent the globe, on whose each side we trod,
  Till it was dinted inwards: let him walk
  Alone upon't; I'm weary of my part.          285
  My torch is out, and the world stands before me
  Like a black desert at the approach of night:
  I'll lay me down, and stray no farther on.
VENTIDIUS
  I could be grieved,
  But that I'll not outlive you. Choose your death,   290
  For I have seen him in such various shapes,
  I care not which I take. I'm only troubled,
  The life I bear is worn to such a rag,
  'Tis scarce worth giving. I could wish, indeed,
  We threw it from us with a better grace;     295
  That, like two lions taken in the toils,
  We might at least thrust out our paws, and wound
  The hunters that enclose us.
ANTONY             I have thought on't.
  Ventidius, you must live.
VENTIDIUS          I must not, Sir.
ANTONY
  Wilt thou not live to speak some good of me?    300
  To stand by my fair fame, and guard th'approaches
  From the ill tongues of men?
VENTIDIUS         Who shall guard mine,
  For living after you?
ANTONY        Say I command it.
VENTIDIUS
  If we die well, our deaths will speak themselves,
  And need no living witness.
ANTONY          Thou hast loved me,   305
  And fain I would reward thee: I must die;

297 *least* Q1, W2 (last Q2, Q3, W1)

---

286 *My torch is out* cf. Shakespeare, *Antony and Cleopatra*, IV. xv, 85: 'Our
lamp is spent, it's out!'

Kill me, and take the merit of my death
To make thee friends with Caesar.
VENTIDIUS                                   Thank your kindness.
    You said I loved you, and in recompense
    You bid me turn a traitor: did I think                            310
    You would have used me thus? That I should die
    With a hard thought of you?
ANTONY                          Forgive me, Roman.
    Since I have heard of Cleopatra's death,
    My reason bears no rule upon my tongue,
    But lets my thoughts break all at random out.                    315
    I've thought better; do not deny me twice.
VENTIDIUS
    By Heaven, I will not.
    Let it not be t'outlive you.
ANTONY                          Kill me first,
    And then die thou: for 'tis but just thou serve
    Thy friend before thyself.
VENTIDIUS                     Give me your hand.                      320
    We soon shall meet again. Now farewell, Emperor.
                                              (*Embrace*)
    Methinks that word's too cold to be my last:
    Since death sweeps all distinctions, farewell, friend.
    That's all.—
    I will not make a business of a trifle,                          325
    And yet I cannot look on you, and kill you;
    Pray turn your face.
ANTONY                    I do: strike home, be sure.
VENTIDIUS
    Home as my sword will reach.          (*Kills himself*)
ANTONY                          Oh, thou mistak'st!
    That wound was none of thine: give it me back;
    Thou robb'st me of my death.
VENTIDIUS                       I do, indeed.                         330
    But think, 'tis the first time I e'er deceived you,
    If that may plead my pardon. And you, gods,
    Forgive me if you will, for I die perjured
    Rather than kill my friend.              (*Dies*)
ANTONY
    Farewell. Ever my leader, even in death!                         335

323 *all* Q1, W2 (om. Q2, Q3, W1)
327 *be* Q1, W2 (om. Q2, Q3, W1)

335 *Ever my leader* cf. Shakespeare, *Antony and Cleopatra*, IV. xiv, 102:
    'Thy master dies thy scholar . . .'

My Queen and thou have got the start of me,
And I'm the lag of honour.—Gone so soon?
Is Death no more? He used him carelessly,
With a familiar kindness; ere he knocked,
Ran to the door and took him in his arms,  340
As who should say, 'Y'are welcome at all hours;
A friend need give no warning'. Books had spoiled him,
For all the learn'd are cowards by profession.
'Tis not worth
My farther thought, for death, for aught I know,  345
Is but to think no more. Here's to be satisfied.
        *(Falls on his sword)*
I've missed my heart. O unperforming hand!
Thou never couldst have erred in a worst time.
My fortune jades me to the last, and Death,
Like a great man, takes state, and makes me wait  350
For my admittance.—    *(Trampling within)*
    Some, perhaps, from Caesar:
If he should find me living, and suspect
That I played booty with my life! I'll mend
My work ere they can reach me.  *(Rises upon his knees)*

    *Enter* CLEOPATRA, CHARMION, IRAS

CLEOPATRA
 Where is my lord? Where is he?
CHARMION      There he lies,  355
 And dead Ventidius by him.
CLEOPATRA
 My fears were prophets; I am come too late.
 Oh that accursed Alexas!    *(Runs to him)*
ANTONY     Art thou living?
 Or am I dead before I knew, and thou
 The first kind ghost that meets me?
CLEOPATRA      Help me seat him.  360
 Send quickly, send for help. *(They place him in a chair)*
ANTONY    I am answered:
 We live both. Sit thee down, my Cleopatra:

358 s.d. *Runs to him* Q1, Q2, Q3, W2 (om. W1)

---

353 *played booty* played badly in order to lose a game; played falsely so as to
gain a desired object.
357 *My fears were prophets* cf. Shakespeare. *Antony and Cleopatra*, IV. xiv,
120: 'She had a prophesying fear'.

I'll make the most I can of life, to stay
A moment more with thee.

CLEOPATRA
How is it with you?

ANTONY         'Tis as with a man     365
Removing in a hurry, all packed up
But one dear jewel that his haste forgot,
And he, for that, returns upon the spur:
So I come back for thee.

CLEOPATRA
Too long, you Heavens, you have been cruel to me:     370
Now show your mended faith, and give me back
His fleeting life!

ANTONY     It will not be, my love.
I keep my soul by force.
Say but thou art not false.

CLEOPATRA         'Tis now too late
To say I'm true: I'll prove it, and die with you.     375
Unknown to me, Alexas feigned my death;
Which, when I knew, I hasted to prevent
This fatal consequence. My fleet betrayed
Both you and me.

ANTONY     And Dollabella?

CLEOPATRA         Scarce
Esteemed before he loved, but hated now.     380

ANTONY
Enough: my life's not long enough for more.
Thou say'st thou wilt come after: I believe thee,
For I can now believe whate'er thou say'st,
That we may part more kindly.

CLEOPATRA     I will come:
Doubt not, my life, I'll come, and quickly too;     385
Caesar shall triumph o'er no part of thee.

ANTONY
But grieve not, while thou stay'st,
My last disastrous times:
Think we have had a clear and glorious day,
And Heaven did kindly to delay the storm     390
Just till our close of evening. Ten years' love,
And not a moment lost, but all improved
To th'utmost joys: what ages have we lived!

379–80 *Scarce . . . now* ed. (printed as 1 line in Q1)

And now to die each other's; and so dying,
While hand in hand we walk in groves below,                    395
Whole troops of lovers' ghosts shall flock about us,
And all the train be ours.

CLEOPATRA

Your words are like the notes of dying swans,
Too sweet to last. Were there so many hours
For your unkindness, and not one for love?                    400

ANTONY

No, not a minute.—This one kiss—more worth
Than all I leave to Caesar.                    (*Dies*)

CLEOPATRA

Oh tell me so again,
And take ten thousand kisses for that word.
My Lord, my Lord: speak, if you yet have being;                    405
Sigh to me, if you cannot speak, or cast
One look. Do anything that shows you live.

IRAS

He's gone too far to hear you,
And this you see, a lump of senseless clay,
The leavings of a soul.

CHARMION                    Remember, Madam,                    410
He charged you not to grieve.

CLEOPATRA                    And I'll obey him.
I have not loved a Roman not to know
What should become his wife—his wife, my Charmion,
For 'tis to that high title I aspire,
And now I'll not die less. Let dull Octavia                    415
Survive to mourn him dead; my nobler fate
Shall knit our spousals with a tie too strong
For Roman laws to break.

IRAS                    Will you then die?

CLEOPATRA

Why shouldst thou make that question?

413 *become* Q1, W2 (Become of Q2, Q3, W1)

---

394–7 *and so . . . ours* cf. Shakespeare, *Antony and Cleopatra*, IV. xiv, 51–4:
          Where souls do couch on flowers, we'll hand in hand,
          And with our sprightly port make the ghosts gaze.
          Dido and her Æneas shall want troops,
          And all the haunt be ours.
414 *high title* cf. Shakespeare, *Antony and Cleopatra*, V. ii, 285–6: 'Husband,
          I come./Now to that name my courage prove my title!'
415 *dull Octavia* See note on ll. 423–5.

IRAS
  Caesar is merciful.
CLEOPATRA          Let him be so                          420
  To those that want his mercy; my poor lord
  Made no such covenant with him to spare me
  When he was dead. Yield me to Caesar's pride?
  What! To be led in triumph through the streets,
  A spectacle to base plebeian eyes,                     425
  While some dejected friend of Antony's,
  Close in a corner, shakes his head and mutters
  A secret curse on her who ruined him?
  I'll none of that.
CHARMION          Whatever you resolve,
  I'll follow even to death.
IRAS                    I only feared                     430
  For you, but more should fear to live without you.
CLEOPATRA
  Why, now 'tis as it should be. Quick, my friends,
  Dispatch; ere this, the town's in Caesar's hands.
  My lord looks down concerned, and fears my stay,
  Lest I should be surprised;                             435
  Keep him not waiting for his love too long.
  You, Charmion, bring my crown and richest jewels;
  With 'em, the wreath of victory I made
  (Vain augury!) for him who now lies dead.
  You, Iras, bring the cure of all our ills.             440
IRAS
  The aspics, Madam?
CLEOPATRA          Must I bid you twice?
                    (*Exeunt* CHARMION *and* IRAS)
  'Tis sweet to die when they would force life on me;
  To rush into the dark abode of Death,
  And seize him first. If he be like my love,

420 *merciful* Q1, W2 (most merciful Q2, Q3, W1)

---

423–5 *Yield ... eyes* cf. Shakespeare, *Antony and Cleopatra*, V. ii, 52–7:
                    Know, sir, that I
      Will not wait pinioned at your master's court,
      Nor once be chastised with the sober eye
      Of dull Octavia. Shall they hoist me up,
      And show me to the shouting varletry
      Of censuring Rome?
442 *'Tis sweet ... me* cf. Daniel, *Cleopatra*, 74: ''Tis sweet to die when we
  are forced to live'.

He is not frightful, sure.                                          445
We're now alone, in secrecy and silence,
And is not this like lovers? I may kiss
These pale, cold lips; Octavia does not see me,
And, oh, 'tis better far to have him thus
Than see him in her arms!

*Enter* CHARMION, IRAS

                         Oh, welcome, welcome.         450
CHARMION
  What must be done?
CLEOPATRA                              Short ceremony, friends,
  But yet it must be decent. First, this laurel
  Shall crown my hero's head: he fell not basely,
  Nor left his shield behind him.—Only thou
  Couldst triumph o'er thyself, and thou alone       455
  Wert worthy so to triumph.
CHARMION                              To what end
  These ensigns of your pomp and royalty?
CLEOPATRA
  Dull that thou art! Why, 'tis to meet my love,
  As when I saw him first, on Cydnos' bank,
  All sparkling like a goddess; so adorned,           460
  I'll find him once again; my second spousals
  Shall match my first in glory. Haste, haste both,
  And dress the bride of Antony.
CHARMION                              'Tis done.

---

454–6 *Only ... triumph* cf. Shakespeare, *Antony and Cleopatra*, IV. xv,
    14–17:
      Not Caesar's valour hath o'erthrown Antony,
      But Antony's hath triumphed on itself.
      CLEOPATRA
      So it should be, that none but Antony
      Should conquer Antony.
458–63 *Why ... Antony* cf. Shakespeare, *Antony and Cleopatra*, V. ii,
    227–8: 'I am again for Cydnus,/To meet Mark Antony'. Daniel,
    *Cleopatra*, 1477–82:
      Even as she was when on thy crystal streams,
      Clear Cydnus, she did show what earth could show;
      When Asia all amazed in wonder deems
      Venus from heaven was come on earth below.
      Even as she went at first to meet her love,
      So goes she now again to find him.

CLEOPATRA
  Now seat me by my lord. I claim this place,
  For I must conquer Caesar too, like him,                     465
  And win my share o'th'world. Hail, you dear relics
  Of my immortal love!
  Oh, let no impious hand remove you hence,
  But rest forever here. Let Egypt give
  His death that peace which it denied his life.              470
  Reach me the casket.
IRAS                Underneath the fruit
  The aspic lies.
CLEOPATRA *putting aside the leaves*
              Welcome, thou kind deceiver!
  Thou best of thieves, who, with an easy key,
  Dost open life, and unperceived by us,
  Even steal us from ourselves; discharging so              475
  Death's dreadful office better than himself;
  Touching our limbs so gently into slumber
  That Death stands by, deceived by his own image,
  And thinks himself but Sleep.
SERAPION *within*        The Queen, where is she?
  The town is yielded, Caesar's at the gates.              480

471–2 *Underneath . . . lies* ed. (printed as 1 line in Q1)

---

466–70 *Hail . . . life* cf. Daniel, *Cleopatra*, 1106–11:
    And you dear relics of my lord and love,
    The sweetest parcels of the faithfull'st lives,
    O let no impious hand dare to remove
    You out from hence, but rest you here for ever.
    Let Egypt now give peace unto you dead,
    That living gave you trouble and turmoil.
472 *kind deceiver* cf. Daniel, *Cleopatra*, 1504: 'Looking among the figs, finds
    the deceit'.
473–5 *Thou . . . ourselves* cf. Daniel, *Cleopatra*, 1533–6:
    Therefore come thou, of wonders wonder chief,
    That open canst with such an easy key
    The door of life; come, gentle, cunning thief,
    That from ourselves so steal'st ourselves away.
475–9 *discharging . . . Sleep* cf. Daniel, *Cleopatra*, 1517–21:
    Better than Death Death's office thou dischargest,
    That with one gentle touch canst free our breath,
    And in a pleasing sleep our soul enlargest,
    Making ourselves not privy to our death.

CLEOPATRA
He comes too late t'invade the rights of death.
Haste, bare my arm, and rouse the serpent's fury.
　　　　　　　　(*Holds out her arm, and draws it back*)
Coward flesh,
Wouldst thou conspire with Caesar to betray me,
As thou wert none of mine? I'll force thee to't,　　　　　485
And not be sent by him,
But bring, myself, my soul to Antony.
　　　　　(*Turns aside, and then shows her arm bloody*)
Take hence; the work is done.
SERAPION *within*　　　　　　　　Break ope the door,
And guard the traitor well.
CHARMION　　　　　　　　　The next is ours.
IRAS
Now, Charmion, to be worthy　　　　　　　　490
Of our great Queen and mistress.　(*They apply the aspics*)
CLEOPATRA
Already, Death, I feel thee in my veins.
I go with such a will to find my lord
That we shall quickly meet.
A heavy numbness creeps through every limb,　　　495
And now 'tis at my head; my eyelids fall,
And my dear love is vanished in a mist.
Where shall I find him, where? Oh turn me to him,
And lay me on his breast!—Caesar, thy worst.
Now part us if thou canst.　　　　　　　　(*Dies*)

　　IRAS *sinks down at her feet and dies;* CHARMION *stands
　　behind her chair, as dressing her head. Enter* SERAPION, TWO
　　　　　　PRIESTS, ALEXAS *bound,* EGYPTIANS

TWO PRIESTS　　　　　　　　Behold, Serapion,　　　500
What havoc Death has made!
SERAPION　　　　　　　　　'Twas what I feared—
Charmion, is this well done?

491 *our* Q1, W2 (Your Q2, Q3, W1)
500–1 *Behold . . . made* ed. (printed as 1 line in Q1)

---

483–5 *Coward . . . mine* cf. Daniel, *Cleopatra,* 1596–8 '"False flesh", said
　　she, "and what dost thou conspire/With Caesar too, as thou wert none
　　of ours,/To work my shame, and hinder my desire?"'
487 *But . . . Antony* cf. Daniel, *Cleopatra,* 1187: 'Myself will bring my soul
　　to Antony'.

CHARMION
Yes, 'tis well done, and like a queen, the last
Of her great race. I follow her.           (*Sinks down; dies*)
ALEXAS                              'Tis true,
She has done well. Much better thus to die           505
Than live to make a holiday in Rome.
SERAPION
See, see how the lovers sit in state together,
As they were giving laws to half mankind!
Th'impression of a smile, left in her face,
Shows she died pleased with him for whom she lived,           510
And went to charm him in another world.
Caesar's just entering: grief has now no leisure.
Secure that villain as our pledge of safety
To grace th'imperial triumph. Sleep, blest pair,
Secure from human chance, long ages out,           515
While all the storms of fate fly o'er your tomb;
    And fame to late posterity shall tell,
    No lovers lived so great, or died so well.

506 *Rome* Q1, Q2, W2 (Roman Q3, W1)
516 *o'er* Q1, Q2, W1, W2 (e'er Q3)

509 *Th'impression ... face* cf. Daniel, *Cleopatra*, 1643: 'And in that cheer
    th'impression of a smile'.

# EPILOGUE

Poets, like disputants when reasons fail,
Have one sure refuge left, and that's to rail.
Fop, coxcomb, fool, are thundered through the pit,
And this is all their equipage of wit.
We wonder how the devil this difference grows          5
Betwixt our fools in verse, and yours in prose;
For, 'faith, the quarrel rightly understood,
'Tis civil war with their own flesh and blood.
The threadbare author hates the gaudy coat,
And swears at the gilt coach, but swears afoot;        10
For 'tis observed of every scribbling man,
He grows a fop as fast as e'er he can:
Prunes up, and asks his oracle, the glass,
If pink or purple best become his face.
For our poor wretch, he neither rails nor prays,⎫      15
Nor likes your wit just as you like his plays:  ⎬
He has not yet so much of Mr Bayes.             ⎭
He does his best, and if he cannot please,
Would quietly sue out his writ of ease.
Yet, if he might his own grand jury call,              20
By the fair sex he begs to stand or fall.
Let Caesar's power the men's ambition move,
But grace you him who lost the world for love.
Yet if some antiquated lady say,
The last age is not copied in his play,                25
Heaven help the man who for that face must drudge,
Which only has the wrinkles of a judge.
Let not the young and beauteous join with those,
For should you raise such numerous hosts of foes,
Young wits and sparks he to his aid must call:         30
'Tis more than one man's work to please you all.

13 *his oracle, the* Q1, Q2, Q3, W2 (the oracle his W1)

---

17 *Mr Bayes* the name under which the duke of Buckingham satirized
   Dryden in *The Rehearsal* (1671); see Introduction, p. xxi.
21 *Fair sex* cf. *Tatler*, no. 10 (3 May 1709): '. . . there cannot be a greater
   instance of the command of females, than in the prevailing charms of the
   heroine in the play . . . called *All For Love, or The World Well Lost*. The
   enamoured Antony resigns his glory and power to the force of the attrac-
   tive Cleopatra, whose charms are the defence of a diadem against a
   people otherwise invincible'.

*Printed in Great Britain by Fletcher & Son Ltd, Norwich*